M000310761

LIVING LIKE A
LEADER

HAROLD LOWE

Harold
Low

All rights reserved. This book or any portion thereof may not be repro-
duced or used in any manner whatsoever without the express written
permission of the publisher except for the use of brief quotations in a book
review.

Print ISBN: 978-1-54397-665-6

eBook ISBN: 978-1-54397-666-3

TABLE OF CONTENTS

PROLOGUE

These days, most schools are only teaching students how to follow a path or a curriculum, but not teaching them how to lead. I'm sure people have told you that you're a natural-born leader or have leadership qualities, but nobody has offered you step-by-step advice on how to take that natural potential and grow into a great leader. This book is designed to give you all the tools you need. I may talk about a few things you already know, but I'll be introducing you to new ideas and guide you in how to put all of those talents and skills together to become an intentional and effective leader.

Many of you reading this book have been blessed with great speaking abilities, the gift of influence, the talent to relate to other people, the ability to build strong connections, and other unique abilities. I don't want you to squander those natural talents, so we've written this book in a way that will help you to optimize those skills as well as help you to connect the dots and learn new techniques on this long road to influential leadership with concepts that will apply to every aspect of your life. Most importantly, I will guide you in the right direction on how to lead people to be something greater than they ever imagined. It is imperative as a leader that you put other people's needs above your own. As the people around you grow, you will continue to grow as a leader.

With that in mind, I can't overstate how important it is to be intentional every step of the way along your journey. You can't rely on chance or good luck to become a great leader; you need a trained mind with attention to detail. You must be very deliberate and dedicated to growth and learning every day for the rest of your life. Committing to continuous learning will guarantee you a life of never-ending growth and prosperity.

From the beginning, this book will help you recognize what a leader is – and is not – and will lead you on a path with instruction and direction to a goal that begins and ends with discipline. Outlined in each chapter are key themes followed by the methods you need to grow and be successful. Each should be studied and worked on in the order that is written. You can't spend too much time in any one area and neglect another if you want to grow into a well-rounded and well-versed leader.

So settle in, take notes, and let me show you how to become the global leader you always knew you could be!

CHAPTER 1

YOUR BEGINNING

"Leadership is about mapping out where you need to go to 'win' as a team or an organization; and it is dynamic, exciting, and inspiring."[1]

You may have been told you're a "natural-born leader," but how do you expand upon that natural ability to become a skilled leader?

If you're reading this book, you have big dreams, but you've probably already realized that your natural leadership ability will only get you so far in the world. You understand that, while having natural talent is a great place to start, there are many skills involved in becoming a great global leader. You're eager to learn, and I want to help show you the tools you need to grow from being a person that others naturally follow into a truly intentional global leader. The great news is that your willingness to learn will take you far as a leader. The fact that you're reading this book means you're serious about doing what it takes to reach your fullest potential.

Be mindful of the fact that everything I say and suggest is for a reason. If you disagree with something, take a minute to think about why. It's OK to disagree, as long as you have valid reasons. Just understand that there is a reason behind everything I mention in this book; nothing is here just for filler.

So let's take a look at some of the skills I will be addressing in this book and why these skills need to be learned rather than relying too heavily on natural talent. While you likely already have some of these skills, it takes knowledge of all of them, how to apply each, and how to combine those skills to become a great global leader. Making goals is something that doesn't come easily for a lot of people, or they think it's okay to keep those goals inside their head. Learning how to make short- and long-term goals will help you decide upon the leadership path you want to take and what steps you need to follow along the way to help you get there.

Without being intentional about setting goals, you're unlikely to become as successful as you could be. It is important to set goals higher than you think you can reach. I believe that it is better to fall short of a lofty goal than to miss your true potential by aiming your sights too low. With that in mind, short-term goals are the steps that will walk you toward your long-term goals and bring you the success that you seek as a leader. I want to show you how to set attainable and far-reaching goals, change them when needed, and achieve them – or at least grow as a person and a leader in the process of failing to reach a goal. After all, each setback is nothing but another learning experience, and becoming a great leader is about constantly learning and growing.

Once you have goals, you need a very specific, detailed, intentional plan of action that will help you reach them. Your plan of action lays out every step you need to take to start reaching those goals. You might be able to reach them without a plan of action, but you're more likely to reach your goals more efficiently and effectively if you have a plan of action in place. You'll also be less likely to fail when you encounter setbacks if part of your plan anticipates setbacks and addresses how you will handle them. The more detailed your plan of action is, the more likely you are to succeed in the long run.

Part of developing your plan of action requires you to understand the difference between "community service" and "service to your community." Understanding why it is important for you to differentiate the two terms will go a long way toward helping you become a great leader and surrounding yourself with the type of people who will help you succeed. While the difference between the terms may seem subtle, there are crucial differences that will affect whether or not people decide to follow your leadership. Without people who are willing to follow you, it's much more difficult to become a leader, so pay close attention when I describe the difference in Chapter 3. I'll also discuss in detail why service to your community is such an important part of becoming a global leader.

As you develop your plan of action to become a leader, you need to base it on your passions. Becoming a leader can be a thankless task at times, so you'll need to rely on your passions to keep you going when it may seem like the rest of the world is against you. It can be difficult to dig deep to discover your biggest passion is, so I want to help you uncover it. I'll help show you how to discover and prioritize your values and use them to pinpoint your passion. Since your passion is based on your values, your passion and values will ensure that you don't accidentally take steps toward your goals that conflict with your moral compass. Your passion will also help you to focus on which priorities are the most important and will help you recognize and attract the type of followers you desire as you reach for your goals.

Speaking of the type of followers you want, it's important to learn how to encourage the people around you to help others and be willing to become leaders themselves. If those under your leadership don't have a true passion for helping others, they aren't likely to stick around for very long. I want you to be able to teach your followers to become leaders so that your organization will thrive. If you lead by example, teaching your followers to become leaders can lead to exponential growth. This will your legacy..

One thing you may not realize you need to learn about becoming a leader is how to develop the proper mindset to continue learning and put everything you learn into a solid plan of action. The wrong mindset will drag you down faster than anything. It takes on-going, positive, intentional thinking to reach your goals; negativity will only hinder your growth, as well as the growth of those around you. A natural-born talent to lead doesn't automatically include the correct frame of thought for being intentional about becoming the best leader you can, so I'll illustrate for you how to develop the proper mindset for tackling this task.

You'll notice that I will often refer to the title of this book, "Be Intentional." What I mean is that you must take it upon yourself to deliberately work on the things mentioned in this book and not just go through the motions. Just like being in a math class, simply showing up to class isn't enough to be a good student; you have to actively take notes, study the lesson, and practice problems to become proficient. Everything you do in life, you must do with purpose. You need to have so much purpose in your thoughts and actions that you believe your goals and dreams are already being fulfilled. Speaking your intentions into the atmosphere with power and acting on those objectives will bring results that will take you by surprise. I'll address this more in Chapter 4, and it's the most crucial skill you'll learn in this book.

One of the most important things about being intentional is that it will help you tune out your detractors. In this day and age, there are trolls around every corner who aim to bring you down for the sole purpose of feeling better about themselves. It is important to recognize that their negativity has nothing to do with who you are as a person. In fact, it has nothing to do with you at all – a doubter is unhappy in their own life and thinks that bringing others down gives them a form of happiness that they can't find elsewhere. Tuning out their negativity will aid in your success.

Being intentional also comes with an added level of faith in yourself to push on despite adversity and tune out critics along your path to success. By being focused and intentional, you can ignore the negativity of others and focus on yourself and your journey. This can be the difference between success and failure. It is your faith and your passion that will help carry you through the hard times in life.

Your support system will be critical during your journey. These are the people you'll be able to lean on when times are tough, who will pick you up when you're feeling down, and who will challenge you when they feel you aren't bringing the best or most practical ideas to the table. I'll show you how to decide who does – and does not – belong in your support system and how you can best utilize them. A good leader is only as strong as the people they surround themselves with. That's why your support system is so crucial. Trusting the wrong person to become part of your support system can cause a catastrophic collapse. Your support system will help you identify your strengths and weaknesses. It can be difficult to spot and admit your weaknesses, and it's too easy to overestimate your strengths. Your support system can help you be more honest than you would be if you tried to analyze your strength and weaknesses alone.

For example, one of your weaknesses, your level of financial literacy. Being financially literate is one of the most overlooked aspects of being a great leader, and today's school system is behind the times when it comes to teaching our youth how to generate, manage, grow, and invest their money. You may not even realize how little you know about managing your money. Financial security allows leaders to spend more time serving their community and building leadership capacity in others. If you are looking for the quickest, most efficient way to become financially stable, I will show you what you need to know to make the most of your money so that you can spend more time focusing on other aspects of becoming a leader instead of struggling to make ends meet. Even if you think you have budgeting down to an art form, be sure to pay attention to Chapter 5.

I should note, however, that money is a tool for becoming a great leader. Becoming a leader should not be a tool to pursue money. As I talk about financial literacy, nothing I mention is meant to get rich quick; as with everything in life, it takes time to build quality. Shortcuts and half-doing things for quick success only lead to even quicker downfalls, so be sure that you add value and quality to everything you do, especially in regards to your finances. Great leaders should shift their thoughts from making a million, to serving a million.

Another aspect of being a strong leader is understanding how and why you need to grow your brand. Every aspect of your life is under a microscope, and your brand requires constant attention to make sure it's adding to your image as a leader instead of detracting from it. There are a plethora of factors that go into building a brand that go beyond just the surface, things that go beyond just the physical aspect of what people see when looking at you. For now, let's just say that it includes far more than just how you display yourself on your various social media platforms. Maybe you already have a strong brand. Maybe you have little to no brand at all. Maybe you need to rebuild your brand from scratch. No matter what the case may be, you need to start working on it now. It takes a long time to build a strong brand and only one small mistake to tear it to pieces. I'll show you what you need to know to build a solid brand and how to use it to build opportunities.

One powerful and often undervalued step on your path toward becoming a global leader is international travel. It might be something you haven't considered, or it may be something you've done just for fun, but it's important to travel with the intention of growth. If you're going to travel, use the opportunity to grow as a leader, not just for the purpose of knocking site-seeing tours off of your bucket list and bragging to your friends and family with beautiful pictures. Even a vacation can be a learning experience if you allow it to be.

One great way to travel with intention is to go on mission trips. Mission trips are a valuable way to learn how much you've unconsciously overlooked while also serving others. Many people go on mission trips with the intentions of helping and teaching others. My experience has been quite the opposite. Mission trips have allowed me to develop valuable wisdom and skills that have molded my leadership capacity. I have also strengthened my moral compass by cultivating values, such as empathy, team work and love. Learning from other cultures in their natural environment (not just tourist sites) enriches your cultural, political, social, economic and spiritual understanding of global citizens. Although it may sometimes be uncomfortable and maybe even a little scary at times, mission trips do not always go as planned. The benefits you reap are your abilities to develop patience, understanding and flexibility. Mission work is also extremely humbling, which is a key component of being a servant leader.

Now that understand the value of being a global leader, you will need to decide what sort of impact you want to make and learn how to demonstrate that impact everywhere you go. Being a leader is all about positively impacting the lives of everyone you touch. Hopefully you know, you have some leadership skills already, but the more you know about what makes certain people exceptional leaders, the stronger the leader you can become. I will discuss specific examples of great leaders such as Martin Luther King, Jr. John F. Kennedy, and Barack Obama and what made them exceptional leaders.

As you're working on becoming a great leader yourself, it's important to encourage those around you to become leaders also. You can use this tactic to multiply the impact you have on the world. For example, if you teach five people to become leaders, and each of them teaches five people your leadership style, you will have now multiplied your impact to 25 leaders. If each of those 25 leaders teaches five more, you've expanded your reach to 125 people, and so on. Understanding different leadership styles and what makes a great leader will help you reach those first five people to start expanding your influence and build a legacy.

Once you've learned all these skills, it comes down to understanding how to put them all together. All the pieces individually won't mean anything unless you practice and grow them collectively. I'll give you the tools you need to combine everything into one package and plan. If you already have all these skills, you may not need this book. If you are missing any one of these skills, this book can truly help you become the leader you are destined to be!

What is a leader?

"Leaders help themselves and others to do the right things. They set direction, build an inspiring vision, and create something new. Leadership is about mapping out where you need to go to 'win' as a team or an organization; and it is dynamic, exciting, and inspiring."[1]

Everyone has their own unique definition of a leader. You may consider a leader to be somebody who inspires, somebody who teaches, somebody who is a creator, or you may have a completely different idea of what makes a leader. Go ahead and take a minute to come up with five qualities that you think define a leader.

_____

_____

_____

_____

_____

Whatever your definition of a leader, all leaders have certain things in common. I'll talk in more detail later in this book about the differences effective and ineffective leaders and different leadership styles, but for now, I'll say that a leader, at their most basic level, guides and directs the paths of others for a greater good. A leader has a vision for the future, a desire to help their community, and the burning need to inspire others to follow that vision. A leader wants to prompt others to lead instead of just following. A leader is so passionate about their purpose that people follow them willingly without feeling forced. A great leader should also be charismatic and honest.

A leader is not the same thing as a manager. A manager may also be a leader, but not all managers are leaders. We've all had that bad manager who belittled us and cared more about the bottom line than the welfare of the employees they oversaw. While a leader may also be pursuing a bottom line, they care about the people following them and want to pull them up, not drag them down.

You may already be a leader if you have people following you on an upward path. I want to help you become the most effective leader you can be by showing you the tools and skills you need and helping you develop a plan.

Why do you want to be a leader?

This may seem like a simple question, but it isn't one that you should take lightly. Your desire to be a leader should come from a deep-rooted passion for helping others. Your passion will guide the reason why you choose to become a leader. Without a strong "why," there's no point in learning the "how." If you don't know why you want to be a leader and you don't have a true passion for it, then you will come across far too many obstacles to be able to reach your goals. If you have a strong enough "why," you will overcome any obstacle in your way by being flexible about the "how" as new issues arise. The "why" will drive you on the hardest days, when you don't feel strong enough to continue.

Take a minute to list five reasons you want to be a leader here.

_____

_____

_____

_____

_____

Not sure about your "why" yet? That's okay. I'm here to help you figure it out.

Here are some bad reasons to decide you want to be a leader:

-You like to be in control of other people.

Being a great leader isn't about controlling people and forcing them to do things your way. Being a great leader is about encouraging people to see things from your perspective. You will never be able to accomplish that by controlling people. In fact, great leaders want to be able to hand off control of certain aspects of their enterprise to others within their organization instead of retaining all the control themselves. If you have aspects of your personality that tend to be controlling, you may need to rein them in a little bit and focus on your passion, which shouldn't be about control but encouragement.

-You want to have power over others.

Great leaders aim to be respected by their followers. It doesn't work to demand respect by lording your authority over people. A great leader wants people following them voluntarily, not because they feel obligated to bend to their power. Being a leader is about guiding people in a certain direction, not forcing them in that direction. There is a difference between power and influence. Power is about using your authority to force people to do things they might not want to. Influence is about changing people's perceptions and encouraging the right behavior rather than compelling it with power.

-You want to make a name for yourself.

While you may make a name for yourself in the process of becoming a notable leader, that shouldn't be your primary goal. Your primary goal should be to follow your passion for helping others. If you have a noble passion and a strong work ethic, you may very well gain a level of fame, but if fame is your end goal, you will be distracted from your desire to lead and your ability to find satisfaction within yourself. Becoming a leader is about appreciating every step of the way, and if making a name for yourself is your primary goal, you might find misery in the process.

Here are some better reasons to become a leader:

-You see the needs of people around you.

If you have a passion for helping others, you will rarely fail in your quest to become a great leader. Becoming a leader should be about wanting to bring people around you up instead of taking them down to climb your way to the top. Seeing a need and filling that need is a fabulous reason to become a leader. There are a lot of people in this world who need help, and there aren't enough people who are willing to step into leadership roles and help.

-You're compelled by a higher power.

Whether it's God, Jesus, Mohammed, Buddha, Ganesh, the Universe, or your conscience, something is compelling you to become a leader. This is arguably the strongest reason to become a leader. When you feel guided by your higher power, you will let little stand in your way of becoming the great leader you feel destined to become. Whatever higher power speaks to you can help you overcome the many obstacles you will face as you grow into the global leader you believe you can be.

-You have a goal in mind that requires others to build.

Some things can't be done by yourself, and it's okay to admit that. The key is to encourage others to believe that your goal is important enough for them to help you achieve it. Trying to force others to build toward your goal will cause undue struggle on your journey, so you'll want to try to find people who share your passion. No matter how large or small your goal, you will need to encourage others to believe in your goal as strongly as you do.

-You see that others are easily influenced by you and want to follow you, and you're willing to lead them down the right path.

Maybe people are following you already, and you want to take responsibility for them and guide them down a good path. Some people need a lot of guidance in their lives, and if you're willing to lead them down an honorable path, that's a great reason to become a leader. Without your guidance, they may end up on a path they regret travelling.

Are you already a leader? How can you tell?

-Others are easily influenced by you.

If you've ever started a trend, you may have noticed how much other people are impacted by your words and actions. If people want to do what you do, say what you say, and be where you are, then they already see you as a leader. Too many people have a natural influence on their peers and squander that influence by settling for popularity. They have zero intention of guiding anyone around them on any path but down. It's up to you to expand your natural ability to lead and become a skillful leader who can guide people down a productive path. Now is also the perfect time to decide what your intentions are for becoming a leader and make a very deliberate, plan on how best to guide people who are influenced by you.

-You have a specific goal in mind, and others want to help you achieve it.

If this is the case, you are ahead of many of the other people who are reading this book. You're well on your way to becoming a great leader, and I'll give you more skills to help you achieve your goal. If others already appreciate your goal, the skills I offer you will help you take advantage of that sooner rather than later.

-People look to you for guidance.

Are you the person all your friends come to with their problems? They see you as somone who has answers to their problems, or just the right amount of skill to listen to them without judging. If people are already looking to you for guidance, you're already well on your way toward being intentional about guiding people down a specific path with your goals and their best interests in mind.

It's a beautiful thing to see a leader who only has the best interest of the people around them at heart. On this journey, you will see people who only intend to use the people around them as building blocks for their personal agenda, usually stemming from a selfish need for power or immoral gain. These people will fail. Even if their enterprise succeeds, they will have failed to be upstanding humans in the process.

Excited to learn more?

If this chapter helped reaffirm that you want to be a leader, then keep reading to discover your passion and why it's one of the most essential building blocks in guiding you as a leader!

CHAPTER 2

FIND YOUR PASSION

*"Give to us clear vision that I may know where to
stand and what to stand for – because unless I stand
for something, I shall fall for anything."*[2]

Decide who you want to lead and why

I want you to understand that everything you do must
be done with intention. You don't stumble upon becoming a
great leader; you must set out every day with the specific purpose of growing into the best leader you can become. That
intention must come with a very detailed idea about who
you want to lead, why you want to lead them and where
you want to lead them. Without purpose, it will be too easy
to stray off track and become distracted by things that don't
matter in the long run. When times get tough, your "why" is
what will keep you going or may even be the reason that you
get back on track.

While you need to start with a solid plan, you also
need to be open and flexible to changing it. Sometimes, life

happens in the most unpredictable of ways, and you must be ready and willing to account for any changing variables that may arise. You may need to tweak your strategy regularly to account for the fact that life never goes exactly the way you think it will. As long as you keep your passion, values, and end goal in sight, you'll be able to change your plan without changing your end goal.

Many people attack life with no strategy and just go with the flow. That mindset is fine when you're only responsible for yourself, but when other people depend on your guidance, you are obligated to have a more stringent plan of action so that you don't impulsively and unintentionally lead them astray. Being a great leader takes a unique combination of resolve and flexibility to pursue your goals in the face of adversity.

It's true that it's important for all people who wish to be successful to set goals and make plans, but it's even more critical for leaders to have specific goals and plans since they have others relying on them. As things come up, you should always have the people behind you in mind. You should always be wondering, "How will this change affect them?" Being responsible for the welfare of others is a task that you shouldn't take lightly.

Moving ahead without a plan turns into a situation of the blind leading the blind, which can only be a recipe for disaster. I want you to remember that it is your vision that will guide your followers through the most difficult days. That's why it's important to have such a clear, intentional plan reinforced by your passion. With that being said, that passion should be on full display. The more that people see your vision, the more comfortable or inclined they will be to stand by you.

If you aren't sure what your true passion is yet, hang in there. I'm here to help you figure it out. It's imperative that you discover it before embarking on your journey to becoming a leader. Using your true passion as the reason behind your leadership is the best way to ensure that you stay the course without being distracted by other opportunities or discouraged when you encounter obstacles.

Take your passion and funnel it into a target audience that shares and or relates. Not everybody will share your passion, and you don't want to waste too much time reaching out to the wrong groups of people who can't be encouraged to see your vision and share your passion. It's up to you to decide who you want following you and to figure out the best method and location to find those people.

Since you will want your followers to become interested in leading, it's important to select the right kind of people to build around. You will learn over time how to find people who share your passion and will be the most likely to help lead your organization into the future, even after you're gone. That's the surest way to leave a lasting legacy, and it all comes down to picking the right team.

Using your core values to find your passion

You may already know what your core values are, but more than likely, you haven't taken the time to sit down and list all the things that are important to you and rate them by order of importance. If you think about it, you will see that you are the happiest and the most settled when your actions support your core values. Doing or saying things that go against what you truly believe feels terrible and won't help you succeed in the long term.

Here's an example. Let's say your boss asks you to lie about something to get a promotion with a raise. If honesty is one of your top core values, you won't feel comfortable lying to get a raise and a promotion. If earning money is your top core value, you might feel more inclined to lie just to get that raise. Now let's say the promotion offers you the chance to help others in some meaningful way that your current position doesn't allow you. If you hold helping others as a higher value than telling the truth, you might consider telling a lie to have the opportunity to do more good with the promotion.

Life is all about finding a balance, which is where peace lies. Knowing how high or low a value sits on your list will help to make some of life's toughest decisions easier.

I hope this example helps you to understand exactly why it's so important to understand what your core values are and how you need to use them to discover your passion and create your leadership plan based on those core values. Your values will determine every decision you make, so you don't want your goals to be negatively impacted by having a passion that isn't aligned with them.

Here are some tips on figuring out what your core values are and how to rate their importance in your life.

Figure out times when you're happiest. You should use examples from home, work, school, and other areas of your life. Think about what you were doing, who you were with, and what about the moment made you the happiest.

Think about the accomplishments you are the proudest of. Think about why you were proud, if others were proud of you, and what caused you to feel proud.

Think about the times you felt the most fulfilled and satisfied. Decide what about the experience gave your life meaning and felt fulfilling. Think about which needs or desires were fulfilled and what factors contributed to that feeling.

Most importantly, think about the values you were raised upon. Which character traits have you lived your life by? What traits make up your character?

See Figure 1 for a list of possible values. Circle the ones that call out to you as being important. Pick your top ten and list them in order of importance here.

_____

_____

_____

_____

_____

Figure 1

balance	experience	originality
authenticity	excitement	organization
challenge	freedom	passion
competency	generosity	pleasure
competitiveness	helping society	poise
confidence	influence	productivity
connection	innovation	professionalism
consistency	inspiring	purpose
continuous improvement	integrity	quality
contribution	intelligence	religion
control	justice	reputation
cooperation	knowledge	significance
creativity	lawfulness	spirituality
curiosity	leadership	status
development	learning	structure
dignity	legacy	sustainability
diversity	logic	talent
efficiency	love	tradition
empathy	loyalty	transparency
empowerment	making a difference	trustworthiness
enjoyment	meaning	unity
equality	meaningful work	wealth
ethical	merit	wisdom
excellence		

Once you've figured out what your top values are, you can use these values to uncover your true passion. If your top value is compassion, for example, your passion may be helping those who are less fortunate, maybe by housing the homeless. If health is your top value, maybe your passion will be helping schools in low-income areas grow gardens so that underprivileged children can have access to fresh vegetables. If your top value is preparedness, maybe your passion is giving self-defense lessons to women and children.

Now is the perfect time to sit down and assess your values to discover your passion. Go ahead. I'll wait. When you're ready, hop back into this lesson!

Where do you want to be in the long term?

Without specific long-term goals, you will wander aimlessly. After determining those long-term goals, you will need to figure out what short-term actions will help you reach the long-term goals since they go hand in hand. These short-term goals go a long way in helping you monitor and track your growth as well as keeping a close eye on whether or not you're staying on the path to your long-term goals. As you consistently assess where you stand on your short-term goals, you'll be better equipped to achieve long-term success.

As you think about where you want to be in life, think about where you want to be at age 60, then 50, then 40, then 30 and work backward from there. Goals as they relate to business, family, finances, spirituality, or raising children can be in direct interference with accomplishing each other. You have to be flexible in order to keep your priorities straight that is why you should be continuously revisiting, rereading, revising your goals. Utilizing this method will better help you see the end goal as well as allow you to match up your plans for the short-term future with your hope for the long-term future. All your goals should work together toward a common purpose. At the very least, your goals shouldn't conflict with each other.

Each of your goals should be measurable. So many of us set goals that are left up to interpretation. Failing to create ways to measure your success makes it very easy to lie or make an excuse for yourself about whether or not you accomplished each goal to your full potential. Each goal should have a specific definition of what completion of that goal will look like.

Are you only thinking about professional goals? You need to have short- and long-term goals for every area of your life, not just one. I encourage you to consider your goals for your personal life, your professional life, your development as a leader, your spiritual goals, your health goals, your wealth goals and any other area of your life you want to control, improve, and grow in.

As much as possible, your goals should be tied to your passion and values. By engulfing yourself in your passion, the steps for reaching your goals will spring up fluently. "The starting point of all achievement is DESIRE. Keep this constantly in mind. Weak desire brings weak results, just as a small fire makes a small amount of heat."[1] When you're lying around or daydreaming, start to think about your goals, and you'll be surprised how many ideas will begin to flow. There's always something flooding your mind anyway – why not let it be your dreams and goals? As those goals remain on your mind, you will start to receive inspiration in the form of ideas to accomplish the goals you have set out for yourself.

It's imperative that you openly receive these ideas as they come to you and prepare yourself to act upon them. However, you must learn to differentiate between good and bad ideas and those that take you down the wrong path. Every idea will not be a good one, and every good idea will not be meant for the path that you have set for yourself. Be careful as you entertain these ideas.

While you need to have different goals for each area of your life, you also need to make sure your goals don't conflict with each other. For example, a goal of making a million dollars may conflict with an altruistic goal to help your community thrive. Making sure all your goals align with your values and passion can help ensure that you don't run into conflicting goals. When in doubt about conflicting goals, use your values chart to decide which goal is more important to your set of values, then rework the other one.

I want to encourage you to set your goals high and risk missing the mark rather than aiming low and missing out on your full potential. "Shoot for the moon. Even if you miss, you'll land among the stars."[1]

You'll never know how great you could be if you set your goals too low. Set some goals you think might be unattainable; even if you don't reach them, you're likely to achieve great things while you reach for what seems to be impossible. Setting goals that are too easy to achieve is a sure way to miss out on reaching your maximum leadership potential. More on this in chapter 4.

Once you've figured out your goals, think about helping others around you set their own goals, especially those who spend time around you or look up to you. Part of being a leader is helping others reach their full potential, and they're unlikely to do that without setting a few goals along the way. Setting goals is difficult for a lot of people, so helping others to set their own goals is a great way to set yourself up as a leader. You're only as good as the people you surround yourself with, so helping your followers reach their goals only serves to enrich your organization and make it that much better.

Once you have determined your goals, passion, and values, you can combine all of those things into one concrete plan. It's important to consider what steps you need to take to achieve your goals and how your passion and values will affect those steps. All these things must be in agreement with each other for you to succeed. If there's any conflict between your goals, values, and passion, no plan of action will be able to overcome that conflict.

Creating a plan of action

You may prefer to live life flying by the seat of your pants. Perhaps you feel that passion and goals are enough without creating a specific plan. I would like you to reconsider that opinion. A detailed plan of action created with intention is the best way to ensure your success as a leader.

Without a plan, random events can drastically change your life. That's not to say that those random events won't force you to change your plan. But if you have a plan in place, you will be better prepared to handle sudden events or catastrophes, and you'll be less likely to stray from your ultimate goals.

A good plan of action should try to foresee potential problems and include solutions to these problems. You can't imagine every scenario, but as the clichè goes "poor planning leads to poor performance. Having a few contingencies in place will help make life simpler and keep stress away.

Arguably, the most important thing to remember when creating a plan of action is that you need to write it down and keep it somewhere you will see at least twice a day (when you wake up and before you go to sleep). It takes seeing something 28 times to commit it to memory, so you'll want to make sure you look at your plan of action at least 365 times per year to keep it in the forefront of your mind. This will help you instinctively make decisions that take you closer to your goals. Make your subconscious work for you by forcing it to consider your plan of action every day.

The difference between a dream and a goal is writing it down. No matter how detailed it is, any plan you have in your head is just a dream. To have a true goal, you need to be intentional about writing down your plan of action and keeping it somewhere you can refer to it regularly. You may need to change it often, and that's okay, but it needs to be written down to be a useful guide for you.

You wouldn't trust a map that was only in someone's mind, would you? As you write down your goals, be sure to make a detailed list of steps that will be necessary to attain each goal. As you follow the steps on this list, you will be able to track your progress with the completion of each step. If you have only accomplished half of the steps necessary or you continue to procrastinate on the same step, then you can always see where you stand on that goal. The best thing about tracking your goal step by step is being able to identify where your mistakes or mishaps are. For many of us, it becomes difficult figuring out what continues to hinder us from achieving our goals; in this manner, you can see exactly what the issue is.

"Writing it" doesn't just mean pen and paper – that would be too easy to lose or forget – you want that plan to be everywhere. A note on your phone, tablet, or computer is just fine, and may even be better because it will be easier for you to refer to it on a regular basis. You should even consider having it, or part of it, as the screensaver or background on your phone, tablet, or computer so that you notice it every time you go to use your device.

The ability to look at your plan of action regularly helps you to remain intentional in all your words and actions, which helps you turn your dreams into goals. You may feel that you have your plan memorized, especially if you read it daily (or even several times a day), but there is something powerful about seeing the words and being able to read them aloud. It activates a different part of your brain than just accessing a memory, which gives it a stronger power of intention. Share your goals with someone close to you who you know will remind and encourage you to stay on track. You can show reciprocity by doing the same for them.

The more often you look at your plan of action, the easier it will be to keep it in mind with every step you take in your daily life, meaning each step will take you more directly toward your goals. It's too easy to let your goals slip into the back of your mind, and the next thing you know, you've accidentally done something to damage your brand, and now you need to rebuild it from scratch.

It's important to note that a plan of action requires just that – action. This isn't a wish list. Your plan of action should include very specific actions that you can take to reach your goals. The more steps you can include with the most specific actions you can take, the more likely you are to reach your goals. Don't rely on guesswork and luck to get you where you want to go in life.

I want you to keep in mind the importance of delayed gratification. Even short-term goals can take a while to achieve, and long-term goals are just that – they can require a long time to reach. You may need to put aside things that would make you happy now to get the satisfaction of achieving goals that take time to reach.

We live in a time where we're used to getting things we want nearly instantly. If a web page takes more than a second to load or a Netflix video takes too long to buffer, we lose our cool. Learning to be patient can be a difficult skill to master. This is one reason it's so important to have your plan of action written down. It will remind you to focus on your long-term goals without getting side-tracked by short-term satisfaction.

When you must forgo a pleasure today – such as going out to an expensive dinner with your friends – to reach a goal – like being financially stable enough to focus more on your passion than your paycheck – it can be easy to become bitter about it. When you look at your plan of action to remind yourself of why you are making sacrifices today to accomplish your goals tomorrow, it makes it that much easier to delay gratification and stick to your plan. That's why it's crucial to include a budget with your plan of action. It is of paramount importance that your budget fits your goals in each aspect of your life. Details to come in chapter 5.

Once you have your values, passion, goals, and plan of action all mapped out, it's time to learn the difference between "community service" and "service to your community."

CHAPTER 3

COMMUNITY SERVICE VS. SERVICE TO YOUR COMMUNITY

"And so, my fellow Americans: Ask not what your country can do for you — ask what you can do for your country."[5]

What's the difference?

When you think of community service, you probably think about something you're required to do, like volunteering a certain number of hours per semester for school or being committed to a certain number of hours of community service as punishment for a crime.

While the term "community service" should mean the same thing as "service to your community," these days it connotes not-so-voluntary volunteer work. Community service is well-intentioned, but it usually involves one event or a certain number of hours, and once the requirement is met, community service is abandoned in favor of something else.

I would like to encourage you to think in terms of "service to your community," which is a genuine, altruistic concern for a certain group of people. To become a great leader, you should be passionate about helping others from the goodness of your heart instead of some perceived duty to your community.

Let your heart guide you; if you love children, then find more ways to give your time to children. I have a passion for helping homeless citizens as well as building up my community (what does "building up your community mean?) . So everything I do is either geared towards feeding the homeless or supplying them with necessary materials or conducting events to help give people in my local and global community information or materials that they would not be able to find otherwise.

Community service is an act that you just show up for and leave after your job is done, whereas service to your community requires forethought, planning, effort, and genuine passion. You can feel the difference when you conduct an event and find yourself staying late to continue conversations you had with the people you were helping or even carrying on those relationships beyond the event. For those involved with middle and high school mentorship, you can tell the intention the volunteers by the way they interact with students. The ones that love what they do, put forth the effort to carry on relationships outside of the regularly scheduled sessions.

Service to your community should involve building bridges between individuals and groups, as well as making a lasting impact. It should not be about performing activities because it looks good on your resume or it is required. It should be something you love to do while developing a self-sufficient society. People in need deserve better than a token of your time, they deserve the same effort and adoration that you would want if you were in that same position. Don't rob them of a loving experience. If you don't think you can do that, then maybe that activity isn't meant for you.

Providing service to your community is an opportunity to develop your leadership skills. It is a great way to find people who share your passion that may be willing and capable followers who might strive to become community leaders in their own right.

Where does your passion come into play?

You won't become a global leader overnight. You need to be OK with being a small leader first. Appreciating each tiny step along the way will make the journey toward becoming a global leader that much more enjoyable. Without acknowledging the value of being a small leader, it will be a long slog toward becoming the global leader you strive to be.

Along your path toward global leadership, external rewards may be limited, which is why it's so important to include your passion in everything you do. Building something based on your passion will bring you internal rewards when external rewards come slowly as you grow as a leader. Following your passion in service to your community is a great way to enjoy every small leadership role as you grown, which is one reason I believe service to your community is necessary on your journey to becoming a global leader.

Leading groups on a small scale is an extremely under-rated way of building yourself up to the level you hope to attain. How could you effectively lead the country as the president without having experienced the pitfalls that come with leading smaller groups of people? Leading smaller groups may not feel rewarding at the beginning, especially when you have big dreams; however, doing things the right way early will save you time and headaches in the future.

Why is service important to the process of becoming a leader?

Performing service to your community provides end-less opportunities to learn. You can't grow as a person or as a leader if you stop learning. The opportunities for learning while performing service to your community may surprise you.

I will tell you in Chapter 7 about how a mission trip to Haiti in the wake of the devastating 2010 earthquake taught me a lesson about gaining a greater appreciation for the simple things in life. Things perceived as problems in my own life were minor compared to the problems of the people I met in Haiti – and yet, they all had smiles on their faces, despite how little they had. The intention of helping others became an unex-pected learning experience.

Performing service to your community is the best way to practice your leadership skills. Use this time to plan events, whether big or small. You will be able to see where you can improve and make adjustments. The best part about doing this is that if you make a mistake planning a service event, it will cause little harm. Since you are service-minded, the group you are helping will still receive your love, and the service can still be provided. If fewer people than you expect show up, you run out of materials, or you don't plan accurately for the number of people that attend, you can adjust on the go and make a note of your experience and improve upon these stumbling blocks the next time. However, do not discount the fact that everything you do will be tied to your brand, so give everything your best effort.

The goal is to use your younger years, ages 19-25, to get all the kinks out so that you can learn from your mistakes and be at your best for the rest of your life. Use this time to work on your skills of organization, management, the power of delegation, building structure, communication, problem solving, critical thinking and relationship building. All these skills are essential in running an efficient team. Don't allow yourself to miss out on key skill building.

Organization and structure are key skills that will help ensure that no important details are forgotten while planning an event. Team management, delegation, and management of responsibility are key tools to learn because you can't – and shouldn't – do everything by yourself. Relationship building is extremely important in growing your organization and growing as a leader.

Service also helps you develop a love for helping people, which is what being a leader should be all about. A leader should help the people around them improve their lives while learning to help others in turn. This helps your followers become leaders in their own right, which helps you duplicate your success as a leader. The more leaders you can produce, the farther you can spread your influence.

Since you can't force others to love helping people, the best thing you can do is to lead by example. If you allow your passion for helping others to shine through the people around you will learn to develop and embrace their own true passion for helping others rather than doing it out of a sense of obligation.

Providing service to your community is also a great way to find like-minded people while organizing your events or attending events planned by other people. These people are key to building a powerful network. Hold on tight to people who think like you. You never know when you might see them again or may be able to work with them. Also embrace the opportunity to bond with those that don't think like you, as well as those who possess different gifts and abilities. These individuals will provide unique perspectives and set of skills that will benefit you as a leader and provide a broader impact on the communities you serve.

This is the time to evaluate those around you in a small controlled setting. Have others plan some events or even run the events that you have planned. The only way they will learn is by having to do it themselves. You can view how they react and adapt to adversity as well as see what roles they enjoy. Throwing them into the fire will provide opportunities of reflection which will help them identify and build upon their strengths and weaknesses. Providing leadership opportunities will create a window to see into a developing leader's character. You will know who embraces the challenge of being a leader.

Your character is based on how you treat people who can do nothing for you. Do you treat the homeless with the same respect you would give to a CEO? Are you judgmental? Do you attempt to build empathy and understand the plight of others? A great leader is always ready to listen and learn from everybody they meet, regardless of the situation. Sometimes the greatest lessons in life are gleaned from people you might otherwise consider to be "beneath you" in life. If you listen and observe with intention,, everybody has a lesson you can learn from.

The more service events you have, the more you will see which people are truly involved. The ones who are willing to get their hands dirty with you will surely stick around as you grow. Be sure to notice who really enjoys the work you are doing and who is there "just because," who shows up on time, who is consistent and reliable, who is humble, and how well they collaborate with others. You can do more work with a dedicated team of 5 than an uninspired team of 20.

It would be great to have a group of people who all mesh together immediately and can laugh, joke, and have fun while still getting the work done. Often, it may take a few meetings or events together to build such camaraderie. Whatever you notice, always set aside time to debrief and reflect as a team so that you can strive to get better and tighten up on weaknesses.

Pay close attention to how young leaders behave as individuals and collectively. You will see those who truly enjoy what they're doing, those just doing it because they feel the necessity to be there, those who just want to be a part of something, and even those who were just bored. Some will come to all events, most events, some events, or just one. As you see them conduct themselves their character will be exposed. You will notice the ones who are very humble and love helping others, and those who may be filled with pride, or even uncomfortable. This exposure will help guide how you mentor them individually.

In fact, performing service is the perfect opportunity to learn humility. A true leader should be able to humble themselves when they realize they are wrong or that somebody has a better idea than they do. Humility also prevents you from becoming drunk on power and starting to become a negative influence on people. Serving others provides so many opportunities for growth, learning, and humility that I really can't overstate its importance. Most people think of humility as spending a limited amount of time bragging about your accomplishments. I see it as the ability to put someone else's well-being before your own, being able to not always be in control, and being able to be meek when others say the situation requires brute strength or a brash response.

Instill the love of helping people in those around you

To leave a lasting legacy possible as a leader, you need to inspire others to take the leadership you have shown them and pass them on to the next generation. People who don't have a genuine passion for helping others are unlikely to be willing to take on the mantle of leadership – or they will accept the challenge for less-than-worthy reasons.

Performing service in your community alongside people who share the same interest in helping others will help you meet the ideal candidates for those people that you will want to keep around you. Similar passions and working toward a common goal that will keep your team together.

Think about a company as big as Chick-Fil-A. The reason the employees are friendlier and more helpful than other fast food employees is that those values have trickled down from the top of the organization. If you instill a passion for helping others in all of your followers, it will trickle down and affect everybody in your organization in a powerful and positive way.

Now that you understand the difference between "community service" and "service to your community," let's talk about the mindset you will need to grow into an impact-ful global leader.

CHAPTER 4

THE MINDSET

"Decide what you want. Believe you can have it. Believe you deserve it and believe it's possible for you. And then close your eyes every day for several minutes, and visualize having what you already want, feeling the feelings of already having it. Come out of that and focus on what you're grateful for already, and really enjoy it. Then go into your day and release it to the Universe and trust that the Universe will figure out how to manifest it."[6]

Speak it into existence

What you think about and the energy you cast into the universe comes back to you. Have you ever noticed that the more you think about your problems, the more problems you seem to have? The same works in reverse. The more you think about the things that you want to happen to you, the more likely those things are to happen.

Be intentional with everything you do in your life. You should be saying your goals out loud so often that you start believing that they have already come to fruition. There is power in verbalizing your goals and plans. Not only do they begin to sink deeper into your sub-conscience, but other people can now give advice and lend help because they know exactly what you want. Never be afraid or ashamed to share your goals with others. As a matter of a fact, it is important that you share your goals with those who have the power and resources to help you achieve them. It is also crucial that you share them with those who may become stumbling blocks to you. You want them to know what you are about and where you plan going.

In addition, you should also be looking at your written goals numerous times a day; the more it is put into the other the better chance it has of coming true. This is the best reason to look at your plan of action at least twice a day, every day. Grab a sticky note, and place your goals where you tend to look most often, maybe your bathroom mirror, refrigerator, dashboard, or desk at work. Why not put them everywhere?. The more you see them, the more you tend to think about them. The more you think about them, the easier it will be to visualize the path that leads to your goals.

Be careful what you think

It's crucial to tune out any negativity. Focusing on negativity will only bring you more of the same. Staying focused on what you want will aid you along the path and keep your attention pointing in the right direction. Your thoughts matter more than you realize, so make sure you spend most of your time concentrating on positive thoughts.

"Watch your thoughts, they become words; watch your words, they become actions; watch your actions, they become habits; watch your habits, they become character; watch your character, for it becomes your destiny."[7]

Success must begin with your thoughts, so why not put more energy into controlling and filtering the thoughts that we have? It is so easy to have a negative thought about someone or something. However, those bad seeds can begin to slowly make the whole bunch go rotten.

On the other hand, positive thoughts hold the power to success in leadership because people can feel that energy that radiates off you before you even say a word. Begin to monitor your thoughts; minimize the negative ones, and watch how you will begin to develop healthy habits. Those healthy habits will lead to a healthy life as well as a healthy team. We all know how important mental and physical health is to success. This also goes back to serving your community. (refer to the concept of the book "As a Man Thinketh"). Your thoughts are simply an expression of your heart. Having a heart whose foundation is built on love, forgiveness, humility, understanding, a giving spirit, and gratitude (one of the most life altering expressions) will always lead you to positive thinking.

You only control two things in this life – your attitude and your effort. No one, and I do mean no one, should be able to affect these two aspects of your life. As cliché as it may sound, you should always make a point to put forth 100% effort. If you can't give it your full effort, then why even waste your time or someone else's time? Giving partial effort makes a task take longer and tends to annoy you even more because you look at the clock and you're still working on it. You're the only person who can push yourself; you should never give anyone else that power. What happens when they aren't there to push you? Will you give up? Are you just going to wait for them to arrive? There is nothing wrong with taking motivation from those around you, but it is vitally important that you find control over your effort and put your all into everything that you do.

Admittedly, controlling your attitude is a lot easier said than done. However, it is possible; it just takes some practice. Like anything else, it requires practice and must become a habit. Work on becoming mentally tough. As you climb the ladder of success (and you will find yourself somewhere on that ladder), you will encounter people that push your buttons. Don't surrender power to other people when it comes to controlling your emotions.

More importantly, as a leader, it will be part of your responsibility to calm the team down at times or even to "rally the troops" and bring them back under control when they need it. If you can't even handle your own emotions, others will not see you as a beacon of control. With that being said, your decision-making should always be rational and without emotion.

This is not to say that your decisions can't be based on your feelings toward a specific topic, but they should always be made with a clear mind. Never allow yourself to make split-second decisions because of the way you feel at the moment based on what just happened to you or how someone made you feel. Your personal emotion should be taken out of decisions being made for the good of the team. Do not allow the things that go on in your personal life to negatively impact the well-being of your team. Arguments at home, disputes with friends, and any other issue that does not affect the job at hand should be left at the door and picked up once you leave.

Thoughts turn into words, so you need to be careful about your thoughts. This is the start of the lifestyle you're going to build. Henry Ford said, "If you think you can or can't, you are right". If you continue to think that you can't do something or don't deserve something, then you won't. Build good habits by being careful to keep your thoughts positive. You must train your subconscious to keep success first. What you want should always be on your mind, and taking steps to make it happen should become second nature. You should wake up ready to take the next step, the same way you wake up and breathe. The more you think about success and the things you love, the more you will do them automatically without being prompted. Nobody should have to make you work towards your goals every day.

Changing the way that we think can be difficult. I highly recommend the idea of auto-suggestion to train your mind. This is the action of mentally preparing your subconscious to work for what you want. Your mind is such a powerful tool and must be utilized to its full capacity. The process is as follows:

1 – Write down your goal, in detail.

2 – Write down your plan to attain that goal.

3 – Read over this list when you wake up and before you go to sleep. I recommend taking 10-15 minutes every day to repeat your plan to yourself aloud.

As these ideas become second nature, your mind will start putting these ideas first, which will formulate into words, actions, and habits.

This is another one of the reasons I suggest putting your written plan of action somewhere you can look at it every single day. The more you see your plan, the more you begin to focus on it; the more you focus on your plan, the more likely it is to happen.

Apply each positive thing to every aspect of your life

One important aspect of being intentional is making sure that you are consistent with your efforts in every area of your life, not just the ones you deem the most important. More specifically, you must apply a strong work ethic to every aspect of your life. You can't just work hard at your job while neglecting school. You can't neglect your job while putting in service to your community.

Part of building your brand, which I'll discuss more later, is ensuring that you're the best version of yourself at all times. Allowing yourself to fall into bad habits in one aspect of your life can make it too easy for those bad habits to bleed into other areas of your life. It only takes one person seeing you slack off in one part of your life to ruin your entire brand, and as I'll discuss later, it's very difficult to rebuild a damaged brand.

That's why it's important to be intentional about every part of your life while growing into a great global leader. Any slip could impact your path as a leader in ways that you can't foresee. Also, allowing negativity to creep in anywhere will affect goals in other areas of your life, so focus on applying your powers of positive thinking to everything.

Consistency is key. They say that practice makes perfect, but the truth is that perfect practice makes perfect. Do your best at all times and remain consistent for the best results.

You must have faith in yourself because not everybody will support you

In this world of haters and internet trolls, there will always be somebody trying to put you down in an attempt to feel better about their own lives. If you have enough faith in yourself and your mission to lead, then these people will turn into noise in the background that you can ignore.

Certainly, this can be easier said than done, which is why I've included it in the chapter on having the right mindset to become a leader. As I've mentioned, focusing on your goals, looking at your plan of action, and imagining your goals as if they have already happened can all help you keep your eyes on the end goals without getting distracted by people who only want to bring you down.

It takes a strong amount of faith in yourself, your goals, and your passion to keep you going during the most difficult of times. This is one area where your support system can have a strong impact on your life. When you start to feel negatively impacted by haters, your support system can remind you about your strong points and the positive things that you have accomplished and are planning on accomplishing. They can lift you up when you're feeling low.

Having said that, no amount of positivity from your support system can replace how you truly feel about yourself. Spend a little bit of time at the end of every day writing down your accomplishments. This is one way to stay in a positive head space and have faith in yourself because you are taking the time to focus on your strong points instead of what you may perceive to be your downfalls. Other things that may help you relax and tune out negativity include performing deep breathing exercises or practicing meditation.

Building an unshakeable faith in yourself will see you through a lot of hard times.

Who can you rely on as your support system?

As I mentioned earlier, one thing that can help you maintain that faith in yourself and your goals is your support system – the people in your life who will stand by your side through everything, both the good and the bad times. Mark Twain said, "Keep away from people who try to belittle your ambitions. Small people always do that, but the really great make you feel that you, too, can become great."[8] Reflects who you should include in your support system and why they are so crucial to your long-term success. Beware of keeping negative people around you. Whether or not it's intentional, they can bring you down. Spend more time around people who make you feel worthwhile, important, and capable of following your passion.

Your support system will be people who you can confide in and express your deepest emotions.. It's the people who will always love you, even if you fail, and they will be brutally honest with you when necessary. This may include your family, friends, religious leaders, teachers, and with anybody else who you have a close, trusting relationship with.

Your closest confidants should be included in your support system. To a certain extent, this may include your mentors and mentees. While you may not become close personal friends with them, there should be a personal relationship there. There should be no secrets between you and your support system.

Your support system may (and probably should) change over time. People will come and go throughout your life, and you will need different types of support at different stages of your life. You may be forced to let go of people who are no longer supportive of you for whatever reason, and, hopefully, you will continue developing relationships with people that you would like to include in your support system.

Another important relationship in your life will be with your mentors. Mentors are extremely important people to have in your life as you grow into a global leader. Mentors are there to guide, teach, and lead you. You should have different mentors for every area of your life, from personal to spiritual to work to leadership and more.

You should look for mentors based on their experience in whatever field of interest you are seeking guidance, so you should have a plethora of mentors who you can ask different questions. Relationships with mentors should be built organically and not feel forced. You will have different levels of comfort in what you can and can't express to each.

As the relationship with your mentor gets stronger, who reaches out to whom may change, but it is good practice for those looking to obtain mentors to continue reaching out unless there is an ongoing lack of a response. The people that you want to mentor you are often busy and may forget to get back to you at times; your constant effort will be recognized. A mentor will give guidance and information, but the mentee typically takes the extra step, especially at the beginning.

Some mentors may be in your support system if they become very close with you, but that may not always be the case, and that's okay. Mentors will hopefully not just tell you how to lead and be successful, but show you. Mentors will also help you learn from their mistakes and the mistakes of their mentors. "It is said that only a fool learns from his own mistakes, a wise man learns from the mistakes of others."[9]

Sometimes, people will latch onto you or may feel compelled by you. These will become your mentees. This is another important relationship because the more you teach others, the better you learn those lessons and retain that information yourself. Having mentees also ensures that the success of your vision will multiply as your mentees eventually become mentors in their own right and take on mentees of their own.

It is important to note that the relationship with your mentee can't be one-sided, it must be a personal and mutually beneficial relationship. They may not necessarily become a close personal friend of yours, but they should have a personal connection with you. Your mentee should be able to see as much of your daily dealings as they like, although boundaries must be set based on the relationship you have with that person.

The mentee controls these relationships because they grow or shrink by the level of need by the mentee. Their involvement and effort in reaching out to you determines how far the relationship goes. As a mentor, you are there to give as much guidance as necessary, but only they can control how much help they want from you. If they ask a lot of questions, then you provide a lot of answers. If they call you sparingly, then follow their lead.

Early in the relationship, your mentee must be sending emails and calling you. If you give them a task, see how they handle it. Don't waste time mentoring somebody who doesn't want to take time to communicate with you. The relationship should grow naturally.

Do not over-exert yourself on the mentee; they must want to be mentored. Mentees should take an interest in you and pursue your knowledge. People will ask for your guidance when they see fit.

You should be aware that you will have different relationships with your mentees versus your mentors, and that will require different actions with each group. For example, there are behaviors that mentees should never see, which also ties into your brand. All it takes is for one mentee to see you having an emotional outburst after having a bad day to ruin your brand, leaving you scrambling to rebuild it.

Building on your strengths and weaknesses

It's important to analyze yourself regularly to determine your strengths and weaknesses. This is the only way to grow, both as a person and as a leader. It is imperative that you focus on your strengths and continue to make those stronger. However, it is important that you are aware of your weaknesses so that you can avoid situations that take advantage of those skills that you are weak in. You will want to bring people around you who are strong where you are weak to ensure that your team is well-rounded. As well as making an effort to work on those weaknesses, for you to reach your full potential, you will want to turn those into strengths. Remember, the only thing standing in your way is you.

Since it can be difficult to spot your strengths and weaknesses, it's useful to rely on your support system to help you out. They know you better than you know yourself sometimes and will likely have a more objective view than you. Don't get defensive about your weaknesses. Understand that your support system is helping you by pointing them out so you can work to improve upon them. With that in mind, you should regularly solicit advice from the people around you and consider their ideas and feedback. It's better to find chinks in your armor before you go into battle, and it's equally important to find typos or flaws in your logic before important meetings occur or decisions are made.

This is one area where humility is especially important. People with different life experiences will have different opinions and may be able to point out flaws you haven't noticed. Accept their suggestions humbly – an ego can be your worst enemy and hold you back from changes that could take you to the next level. As a leader, you should always be striving to learn more, and that includes learning from the experiences of others. Brilliant ideas can come from the most surprising people.

Failing to solicit advice can cause you, as well as others, to travel down the wrong path, which can be difficult to recover from. When you have others depending on you and your expertise, it's more important than ever to be aware of your strengths and weaknesses and listen to the advice of people in your support system. It's one thing to ruin your own life with a rash decision – it's another thing entirely to negatively impact the lives of others around you due to a lack of humility and poor decision-making.

One great example of somebody who constantly works on their strengths and weaknesses is LeBron James, a basketball player for the Cleveland Cavaliers, who is regarded by many as one of the greatest NBA players of all time. When he first joined the NBA, he was a powerful slasher and playmaker, but he didn't have much of a jump shot, and his post moves needed work. As he continued to improve his jump shot, he never stopped slashing to the rim or developing his post game. He's always improving on each skill, but in the off-season, he gives special attention to the weak parts of his game. As he developed into an NBA veteran, he excelled in all facets of the game.

Note that it took years of practice to turn a set of skills that were once liabilities into skills that have helped to turn him into, one of the best players to ever play the sport. What cannot be underestimated is the time it took to improve as well as the extreme scrutiny that he received along the way. As a leader, you are embarking on a similar path that will test your mental toughness and tenacity. When things get tough, and everything seems to be working against you, will you quit or rise to the challenge?

What makes a good leader?

According to Task Que, there are 10 qualities that separate good leaders from bad leaders.[10]

1 – Honesty and Integrity

People must have unwavering trust in you. This means you must always be upfront and honest with those around you as well as being notorious for doing what you say you will do. Few things can make someone lose faith in you faster than by not being a man or woman of your word. The 34th President of United States, Dwight. D. Eisenhower, once said, "The supreme quality of leadership is unquestionably integrity. Without it, no real success is possible, no matter whether it is on a section gang, a football field, in an army, or in an office."[11] If you want to be able to trust that those following you are honest, you need to model honesty yourself.

2 – Confidence

If you sound unsure as a leader, people will hesitate to follow you. If you want others to have confidence in your ability to lead, it's important to display confidence in your ability. You need to build yourself up before you can build up others. It has been said that if you say something with enough confidence, then people will believe whatever you say.

3 – The ability to inspire others

Without the ability to inspire others, there won't be very many people to follow you. This is another place where your passion comes into play. If your passion shows through in everything you do, it will help inspire others that share your same passion. Nobody will be inspired by a wishy-washy leader who seems unsure of themselves and their leadership skills. A combination of confidence and passion will make you a force to be reckoned with when your agenda is authentic.

4 – Passion and commitment

We've already talked extensively about how your passion, and your commitment to it, are so important to the process of growing into a global leader, so this one shouldn't surprise you.

Your followers should be able to see your passion and commitment in a way that inspires them to embrace your passion as their own. Nobody should ever have any doubts about your commitment to your team.

5 – Good communication skills

If you can't communicate what you want others to do, how can you expect them to do what you need them to? You may think you are communicating your desires to the people who follow you, but if you're getting inconsistent results, this may be an area you need to work on. It's important to assess whether you are specific enough and direct enough to ensure that you are easily understood.

There's more to having good communication skills than you might expect. You should speak about everything you see your team do. Congratulate the good, and embrace the bad so that you all may learn from it. Your team should always know how you feel. If the goal is to get better, then you must put everything on the table, which is why there is no place for emotions when important decisions are being made.

6 – Great decision-making

Decision-making is tied to confidence that you have in yourself and your team. The best leaders take the time to consider every angle and get advice from others (like your support system) before making any decision that affects others. Once you've made your decision, you must stand by it.

7 – Accountability

While it's easy to brush things off as being somebody else's fault or something out of your control, a great leader will admit culpability and take steps to address problems. Not only is it important to hold yourself accountable for your actions and decisions, but it's also important to hold those under you accountable as well. After all, the actions of those under you reflect on your leadership skills in the end.

8 – Delegation and empowerment

As your organization grows, it will be impossible to do everything yourself. It's important to start working on delegation and empowerment before you reach a stage where it's necessary. After all, giving others responsibility is the only way to see whether or not they can handle it. Empowering others is also a great way to build them as leaders in their own right.

9 – Creativity and innovation

Creativity and innovation are probably the most overlooked items on this list. These two things will give you a leg up on any competition and help grow your organization. Being creative could help you do things more efficiently. Innovation could be crucial to solving problems. For example, innovations like the Life Straw© are helping bring access to clean water to people around the world. Creativity and innovation are required to bring forth positive change.

10 – Empathy

People won't follow you for very long if they feel like you don't care about them. John Maxwell states, "People do not care how much you know until they know how much you care." It's crucial to understand the problems and pain of everybody around you. You must be empathetic to the emotions of others, but you can never let your own emotions get in the way of your mission. Emotions cloud judgment and logic. Allow your support team to see that emotion and gauge how much of it you should express. Sometimes emotions are just temporary, and you can't let temporary emotions compel actions that can leave lasting effects.

You must be able to separate your emotions from the task at hand. It is fine to be emotional, but you should never let that short-term emotion determine long-term decisions. Don't bring your emotions into work, and don't make emotional decisions. You shouldn't bring problems from home to work; it will distract you and negatively affect those around you and impact the task at hand. You especially shouldn't let an argument or a dispute with anyone on your team incite a rash decision that will affect others.

Imagine you're working in a soup kitchen, and there's only enough food for 500 people. You may feel bad for the homeless and try to give them extra portions. While those people will fare better, others may get fewer portions or no food at all. You may have positively affected some people, but at the expense of others. This is the perfect example of emotions getting in the way of your better judgment.

Character is another important – if not the most important – quality of being a good leader. Character is built through learning from your mistakes and understanding that the only thing you can control is your attitude and effort. Character should not be constructed by how others respond to your actions.

Continuous Learning

It's crucial to be a life-long learner. Reading is the quickest ticket to achieving that goal. You should try to read at least one book per month. Reading helps you grow mentally, improve your grammar, and ensure you're always productive. Don't let this be the last book you read about personal growth. The only way to keep learning about yourself is to continue to ask questions as you keep your head in a book. If you are not improving, what is taking place? One thing that is happening is that someone is achieving your goal for you and reaping benefits that were designed for you. If you plan on leading others through mentoring, you must be striving to learn more and be in a constant state of growth.

Using your imagination

The skill that I am about to discuss comes directly from learning to control your imagination. Muhammad Ali said, "If my mind can conceive it, and my heart can believe it - then I can achieve it." It is typical for new ideas to come to you seemingly out of thin air or at moments when you were not thinking of them. This happens because your brain is always working and something in your subconscious had an urge for this idea to come about. How cool would it be if I told you that you could control when these ideas came to you, and you're able to develop them into full concepts or plans?

Controlling your imagination will take practice, but once you've mastered it, you will be able to control your thought process and see all of your ideas fully develop. The next time you lay in bed, close your eyes. Think of 3-5 people who are the most influential in your life, the people that you go to for advice. Imagine them sitting around a dining room table or conference room table, it doesn't matter, as long as you can see all of their faces. The first few times that you do this, start out by saying hello to everyone and hearing their responses back. This will be your measuring stick for how well you developed this room in your imagination. You should be able to clearly see each of their faces and hear their voices when they respond back to you. Keep practicing until you can have a clear conversation with this group. The people you chose should be close enough to you that you know how they respond to certain phrases. You should know how their greeting sounds and how they usually respond to you in conversation. If you cannot do that with each person, then you should pick a new group. This may take a few days to master.

Once you have mastered that first step, you will start your meeting the same way as the prior step. Greet each member of your group and receive their responses back. Then ask a question or introduce an idea that has been on your mind. Subconsciously, the members on your team will begin to provide advice or ideas on the given topic. It should be run just like any meeting you've been to or similar to a Socratic seminar, where ideas are just spread around the room without interruption.

Often the older we get, we tend to use the full capability of our imaginations less and less. This process allows you to use your imagination to put pieces of an idea together. By using the group that you choose, you are now brainstorming, troubleshooting, and creating a rough draft of a concept before introducing it to someone else. Being able to do all of this yourself now allows you to fully develop thoughts that you typically only had bits and pieces of. Utilize the full power of your imagination and develop every idea that comes to your mind.

Your brain is a complex combination of nerves and muscles that together create a beautiful symphony of thoughts and emotions. Being able to control your brain and unlock full access to it will take your thoughts and ideas to a new level.

New Thoughts > New Words > New Actions > New Habits > New You

CHAPTER 5

BECOMING FINANCIALLY LITERATE

"I am concerned that too many people are focused too much on money and not on their greatest wealth, which is their education. If people are prepared to be flexible, keep an open mind and learn, they will grow richer and richer through the changes. If they think money will solve the problems, I am afraid those people will have a rough ride. Intelligence solves problems and produces money. Money without financial intelligence is money soon gone."[12]

You must build yourself up financially, because you may not always be compensated as a leader.

Although I am no expert on finances, I have had the good fortune of learning about money from several people in my network who are wealthy and financially free. These tips are not in any specific order, however, each of them can work to your benefit to reach your financial goals.

When you first start your journey toward becoming a global leader, you may not be compensated with much (if any), so you should work to be financially stable on your own. As a leader, people will look to you for guidance in each aspect of life, so it may be helpful for you to be able to give them some financial advice as well, or at least know where to guide them.

You must begin to develop good financial habits now so that as you begin to see the monetary gain that you hope for, you will know how to handle it. Nothing is worse than looking back on all of the money that you wasted because of your own poor habits. Saving and investing money may seem impossible while you're not making as much as you want, but the habit of setting aside even a few pennies at a time will set you up for a lifetime of success.

To become financially stable, you must learn about saving, investing, building, and planning your income. Sticking to a budget is a crucial part of being able to efficiently manage your income. This is where practicing delayed gratification will come in handy. You'll need to recognize that the thing you WANT to buy today is taking you away from your long-term goals. You may NEED to turn down a lot of desires while you're working on building your wealth, so it's important to keep your end goal in sight.

It's crucial to learn how to use your money wisely so you can spend more time focusing on being a leader rather than bringing in an income, although making money should not start to influence your decisions as a leader. Having money may allow you to live the lifestyle that you hoped for, but being a leader should not be about making money. Being a leader should always be based on your passion for helping others.

Tips

There are two books that I would recommend to anyone who would like to dive more in-depth into their financial growth: *Rich Dad, Poor Dad* and *Think and Grow Rich*. These books go into much more detail about financial planning than I have room for in this book. The more you can learn about managing your money at a young age, the more opportunities you will have as you get older.

On top of reading books about money management, there are many apps you can use to improve your finances like Acorns, Albert, and Personal Capital to help you get started.

Acorns offers tools like letting you round up each purchase you make using your debit card and putting the change into savings as well as regularly transferring money from your checking to savings accounts. This allows you to save money without directly having to put anything aside; you can build up a decent savings account with little to no effort. What I like the most about the app is that it continuously invests the change that is deposited into it, which allows you to begin building your income passively.

Albert analyzes your income, sets aside small amounts of money, and even helps you pay down your debt faster. This app is built as a more traditional savings app, where you can set it up to automatically deposit money into the account. For those who struggle with spending money every time you see some in your account, be responsible and put some away for savings every time you get paid. It also monitors your monthly spending, so you can have a better idea of what your budget should consist of.

Personal Capital helps you track and manage your finances with the help of registered financial planners. You will be able to see all of your accounts at once, as well as closely monitor your net worth. The beauty of this app is that it monitors not only your bank accounts but also your debts, assets, and anything financial that is attached to your name. It also keeps track of your spending and income on a month-to-month basis; in doing so, you can observe your growth throughout the year and make changes to your habits accordingly.

The more time you can spend learning about the best financial practices, the sooner you can become financially stable enough to focus your energy on the activities that you are passionate about. It will take time to build good habits, especially when you factor in the hours it takes to sit down and go through your finances and find the things that you can do better.

Understanding finances may be crucial in your role as a leader, also. If you're running a business, even a nonprofit (ESPECIALLY if you're running a nonprofit), you need to have as much knowledge as possible to manage the money that comes in and out of your organization. It's even more import-ant to understand money management when you're han-dling more than just your own money. Even if someone else handles the finances that you are responsible for, you should be able to double check or verify anything that directly affects you. The actions that you take now will directly impact the future that awaits you.

Budget

The most important part of budgeting is forcing yourself to stick to it. To set yourself up for a lifetime of successful bud-geting, there are a few things that you should consider. The first step is to write your record your budget, preferably in an Excel document, so you don't make an error in counting. A budget kept entirely in your head will eventually fail.

Here are a couple of sample budgets you can use to plan your own budget.

	Budget For the Summer 2018		
Weekly		$500	100%
Title of Expense	Price of Expense		Percent of Weekly Income
1 Food		$30	6%
2 Gas		$50	10%
3 Tithe		$50	10%
4 Misc		$25	5%
5 Financial Freedom		$25	5%
6 Personal Savings		$25	5%
Total		$205	41%
Balance		$295	59%
Monthly		$2,000	100%
Title of Expense	Price of Expense		Percent of Monthly Income
1 Weekly Expenses x4		$820.00	41.00%
2 Vacations (saving up)		$100.00	5.00%
3 Rent		$500.00	25.00%
4 Emergncy Fund		$50.00	2.50%
5 Groceries		$200.00	10.00%
6 Insurance (car, home, life)		$100.00	5.00%
7 Debt (student loans, credit card)		$200.00	10.00%
Total		$1,970.00	98.50%
Balance		$30	1.50%

Or for double the income

	Budget For the Summer 2018		
Weekly		$1,000	100%
Title of Expense	Price of Expense		Percent of Weekly Income
1 Food		$50	5%
2 Gas		$50	5%
3 Tithe		$100	10%
4 Misc		$50	5%
5 Financial Freedom		$100	10%
6 Personal Savings		$100	10%
Total		$450	45%
Balance		$550	55%
Monthly		$4,000	100%
Title of Expense	Price of Expense		Percent of Monthly Income
1 Weekly Expenses x4		$1,800.00	45.00%
2 Vacations		$500.00	12.50%
3 Rent		$1,000.00	25.00%
4 Emergncy Fund		$50.00	1.25%
5 Groceries		$200.00	5.00%
6 Insurance (car, home, life)		$200.00	5.00%
7 Debt (student loans, credit card)		$200.00	5.00%
Total		$3,950.00	98.75%
Balance		$50	1.25%

Outside of the necessities and wants column that will make up your monthly and weekly budgets, you should also look into setting money aside for saving and investing. Many people run into issues with their money because they see all of it in one account and get swipe happy and spend it. It is important to attempt not to allow everything to be spent in your budget. Many people run into problems with their finances because their budget has them spending every dollar that comes in, not allowing for unforeseen events. On top of the money that you put away into savings, there should be money left over in your checking account that doesn't get spent. When this takes place, you will always see your bank account grow.

A great approach is to have more than one account for different purposes. Each checking account comes with a savings account that has no fees; utilize it. If you aren't a W2 employee, you will be responsible for paying your own taxes; they won't be taken out of your paycheck. In that case, you should use a savings account to save money for your taxes. Find your tax bracket based on your income or expected income and set that money aside every time you get paid so that you don't have to worry about not having the money to pay Uncle Sam.

Make a separate checking account for your monthly expenses. This way, you can put money there and not touch anything outside of that one account for bills, groceries, etc. Try using that savings account to set money aside for any investments that you are thinking about. This account may grow slowly or quickly depending on how much money you make and how disciplined you are from spending on personal wants. Let this account grow until you have enough to invest in something that will bring you residual income in the future. Make a point to separate these funds every time that you get paid. Use your budget to decide percentages and amounts that will be distributed into each account.

Finally, use a personal account for everything else, including personal wants and unexpected things that may come up. You will want to always have money readily available in this account so that you never run into situations where you have to transfer money from your other accounts.

A good rule of thumb before buying anything that isn't a necessity is to save up at least six months of living expenses first in case anything goes wrong. People get laid off, homes burn down, or maybe you run into problems with your car. This will give you the ability to not live paycheck to paycheck. Creating this emergency fund will be hard at first, but if your goal is financial freedom, it will be necessary.

Live below your means

This should be self-explanatory. If you don't have it, don't spend it. The goal is to stay out of debt, My mother always told me that if you don't have enough to buy it three times, then you can't afford it. This means that if you don't absolutely need it, then don't buy a new car or new clothes or a home that costs more than your budget allows. Living below your means now allows you to live the luxurious life you want later by saving your money up front. This is where having an extra savings account comes in handy, so you won't be tempted to spend money you should be saving.

Although I recommend buying a used car due to value, if you are going to buy new, don't be tempted into an expensive bells and whistles that will cause debt for years. Do you plan on spending more on an apartment monthly up front or have cheaper monthly payments on a home that you plan to live in for years to come? But, you must also keep in mind that homeowners have certain expenses that renters do not. As we talk about planning, it's time to plan out where you want your money to go for the next 10-15 years. Everything that seems fun now will not benefit you in the future; when it comes to finances, you will always want to think about the future first. Things in life come up unexpectedly so don't get caught unprepared.

Save

Set yourself up for long-term stability by saving money, starting today. Little bits add up over time. Having money saved is very critical for handling any emergencies that may come up at the last minute. Surprise expenses can occur at any time and having to accrue debt hurts more in the long term than being able to use money that you've saved up instead. The more money you can put away before an emergency occurs, the less money you'll have to pay for expensive interest rates on credit cards. Spending money on interest is throwing money out the window.

Start thinking about Roth IRAs and life insurance policies, and put small amounts away throughout the year so that you can begin to save for retirement. Retirement age may seem so far away that you don't feel the need to save for it yet, but the fact is that retiring is expensive. Setting money aside now will help you retire at a reasonable age instead of being stuck working into your eighties or living on whatever social security is left in 40 years. Being able to retire means that you will be able to ensure the same lifestyle and expenses that you have now without having to work for the same income. Start planning on how to sustain your lifestyle for years to come. Then think about what you want to be able to leave for your children; generational wealth doesn't happen overnight.

Look for savings accounts and Certificates of Deposit that offer interest rates to help your money grow while you build up your savings. Finding ways to earn interest is akin to finding free money.

Rainy day fund

No matter what you do with your money, always set aside some money for "just in case." You should always have one savings account that is strictly for emergencies. As I previously mentioned, paying interest (like on a credit card) is like throwing money out the window. You never want to be caught trying to figure out where money is going to come from in times of emergency. The beautiful thing is that if you never spend this money, it just continues to grow as you continue to save.

Don't find yourself stuck without any options when a family member needs surgery, you need to pay for an unexpected funeral, you have to have a tooth pulled because you couldn't afford a root canal and a crown, or you experience other bad news or life complications. Emergencies WILL happen. It's up to you to be prepared to the best of your ability.

Invest

You need to invest your money into things that will bring in a bigger return down the road. Things like stocks, bonds, and real estate won't always pay dividends quickly but will help you build long-term wealth that can even become residual income down the road if done properly. The goal is to have multiple streams of profit coming in every month. This builds an income that you will allow you to be free from working a traditional job.

Look at your budget and see how much money you have available to invest without causing undue strain on your finances. You can either be very aggressive, which brings big gains and the potential for massive losses, or you can be conservative, which brings small gains and minimal risk of losses. That choice strictly comes down to your budget, income, personal goals, and willingness to take big risks with your money. You should also take age into consideration. People under 30 should attempt to be aggressive when it comes to investing. At that age, any amount of money that you invest can be made back up over your lifetime. Everyone's situation is different, but always keep in mind that you will miss 100% of shots that you do not take. With no risk, there is no reward.

If you can't make investments without being comfortable financially, then you aren't ready to invest yet. As that time comes, going into real estate, the stock market, and mutual funds such as a Roth IRA are common practices. Make sure you read up on and research each before you put your money into them. Also, consult people who have found success in these endeavors and pick their brain. Reading is always a great practice. Before I invest my time or money, I am sure to read at least two books on that particular topic. Investing is about taking a calculated risk, so be sure to become a subject matter expert on any risk you are willing to take. Knowledge is your friend. Ignorance will bite you in the butt if you make poor investments.

Build your wealth through residual income

Residual income is the amount of net income generated in excess of the minimum rate of return. This means that once you receive a return on your investment and pay all expenses, you will have money left over, which becomes profit. Money that you make regardless of whether you work or not. If you own real estate, then as long as your tenants pay rent, you will get paid every month. If you have money in the stock market, then every time the stock grows, so does the money you have in it. These things require little to no effort on your part.

This is one of the most important concepts to becoming wealthy. To have your bills paid for without working, you must continuously have money coming in. Everyone hopes to retire at some point, so as you work up to that, you must be working on building your residual income. The sooner you have a significant amount of residual income, the sooner you can retire comfortably.

The lifestyle you want to live will determine how much time, effort, and money you put into this endeavor. Look forward and think about the life you plan to live, then work backward to find the best plan of action to build yourself up to your financial goals. It's worth the investment of your time. You're unlikely to accidentally earn enough passive income to retire.

There will always be bad stocks, and the stock market is not guaranteed, but over years and decades, most stocks usually go up in worth, which means investing in stocks can be a great way to earn residual income as they become worth more while you do nothing.

Bonds are basically loaning your money to the government or a corporation while they pay you back in a set amount of time with interest. These can be another great low-risk way to build residual income.

Net worth

As you begin to attain a certain level of money, your net worth becomes the indicator of what your financial portfolio looks like. Net worth is a measure of your assets minus your debt. Assets consist of your houses (rental properties, not the home you live in), money in the stock market, other property under your name, and so on. Debts will consist of student loans, loans from a bank, and any other money that you owe.

The reason your net worth becomes so important is because it is not a measure of the money in your bank account but the value of investments as well as the money you have in circulation. Most will define wealth as the amount of time you can live without having to work, and your bills will still get paid. Your net worth is a depiction of this in numerical value. The app "Personal Cap," which I mentioned earlier, can aid you in keeping track of this.

Note that if too much of your money is tied up in investments, you can still be "poor" even if you have a high net worth. Keep this in mind while planning your investments.

Taxes

It's imperative that you research and have knowledge of our tax system and how it affects you. Most people don't even know the tax bracket that they sit in and are inevitably just giving money to the government without so much as asking a question.

Take the time to figure out how to minimize the money that you are paying back to the government. That may be through becoming an entrepreneur, utilizing our system of activities that are tax-deductible, or even just taking the time out to set money aside throughout the year for taxes so that you don't go into debt over the money that you earned.

Pay taxes quarterly to avoid a large tax bill in April and have a Certified Professional Accountant (CPA) help you find deductions you may not be aware of. A CPA can even help you plan your next fiscal year to maximize available deductions.

Start early

The earlier you start saving and investing your money, the more financial freedom you can enjoy down the road. It's never too early – or too late – to start managing your money better. All it takes is a little education such as reading self-help books and websites since school trains you to work for other people instead of yourself. The last thing you want is to wake up when you're middle-aged and realize you haven't saved anything for retirement. By then, you will have missed out on 20-30 years of saving up.

Generational wealth

Generational wealth is about more than just money; it also pertains to values and traditions passed down through your family. There are two steps to building wealth for future family members:

Generating wealth is about creating a sustainable income source that will continue to create profit after you are gone. This can include rental properties that you never sell, money in stocks that you never take out, or any other investment that you don't touch and allow to accrue interest.

Giving your children and grandchildren a head start financially is one of the greatest gifts you could give.

Preserving wealth is about keeping the wealth you have generated so that it may continue to be passed down. This typically includes passing assets down to future generations, such as leaving your residential home and vacation homes for your children or setting up trusts and insurance policies that guarantee your children will see the money and assets that you have set aside for them.

As you start a family or start to accrue wealth, it will become crucial to plan what will happen to your family and your money after you die. You never know – you could be struck and killed by a drunk driver tonight while driving home from work.

It's never too soon to create a will, and you should buy life insurance and mutual funds when you get married or have a child. Think very seriously about what will happen to your family when you're gone and plan accordingly.

Financial freedom

The goal for everyone should be to become financially free. This means that you no longer have to rely on working a conventional job. The amount of money that you bring in is no longer determined by the hours that you work. This can come in many forms. You must find your niche and perfect it.

The best thing about becoming financially free is that you can now have freedom with your time. This will allow you to devote key hours to the things that you love. This could mean more time with your family, or more time to devote to your recreational hobbies like golfing or basketball. If you work with any organizations like non-profits, you can now devote more service hours to them. Time is one thing you can never get back; don't waste it doing something you hate because you didn't make the right decisions to prepare for the future.

Money isn't the most important thing in life

Money especially shouldn't be the most important thing in your life when you're focused on becoming a leader. Quite frankly, it should be pretty low on your list of values. Having said that, money is a big part of each of our lives in regards to the way we live.

So take heed to everything listed in this chapter, but there are a few rules that come as you grow financially. These rules were created to maintain your role as a leader without allowing money to take over your mind.

Before you make any purchase, wait at least 30 days before spending your money. By the end of those 30 days, if you still want it, then you probably either need it or deserve it.

As you think of ways to make money, no decision you make should directly or indirectly harm someone. If you go into real estate, you should never purposefully overcharge a tenant or be quick to kick someone out. Remember that your character is still on display. If you can't make financial decisions without it being at some else's expense, then this may not be the lifestyle for you.

Don't allow greed to creep in. Part of the purpose of having your support system is to make sure that you always stay the same person. Do not allow money to change you. As easily as it was given to you, it can be taken away. You should occasionally check in with your support system to see if they think you're being greedy or irresponsible with your money.

Give back. You must continue to give back to your community. I don't usually make it a habit to tell people how to spend their money; however, in this case, I find it necessary. Don't forget your core values as money comes into your life. As I talk about being a leader, giving back should be one of those values.

Teach someone else. As you find success in anything, it is expected that as a leader you help to duplicate that success with somebody else. Money is no exception; along the road to financial success, be sure you teach or give advice to someone who is just beginning their journey. Someone helped you – never forget that. Without question, you need to teach sound financial advice to your children. Create a system so that your children are given financial responsibility as early as possible.

Don't let life lead you; lead your own life

All in all, it's important to make good decisions with your money. Every dollar you spend, save, or invest will impact your future, as well as the lives of your family members. That could be a positive or negative impact, so think wisely about how you're managing your money. Stick to your plan of action, which should include your budget.

The sooner you make a detailed plan for your money, and the better you stick to that plan, the sooner you can take control of your life and live it on your own terms rather than being a slave to money.

CHAPTER 6

YOUR BRAND

"Your brand is what other people say about you
when you're not in the room."[13]

As a leader in the 21st century, the lifestyle you live in your free time will be just as important as your role as a leader.

In today's society, people are looking at your lifestyle just as heavily as the words you are saying. People don't just look at who you are as a leader; they look at your full body of work and the life you live at home. People will observe the way you do things to verify that you practice what you preach; if you don't follow your own advice, then how could anyone else?

Now that everybody has a camera in their pocket at all times, your behavior is constantly under a microscope. If you're having a bad day and take it out on a fast food employee, for example, anybody could record that encounter and put it on the internet, where somebody will recognize you sooner or later, which could tarnish your brand.

Every interaction you have and behavior you display outside the walls of your own home (and the homes of people you trust) are up for public scrutiny and will impact the way that people continue to view you. Whether that's a positive or negative impact depends entirely on you.

Why is your brand important?

Your overall brand is significant because people will always talk about you when you aren't around. When your values carry over from your personal life into your leadership style, you get to control the narrative of what is said about you. If your brand is saturate with good values, people can't tarnish your image, even if they don't like you.

People should always know about the good things you're doing in the world and should never see things that conflict with your brand. The best way to protect against that is not to conduct any activities that contradict the words life you portray. The public eye will create their own opinions and interpretations of you based solely on what they see and hear. Posting quotes and pictures on social media that conflict with your brand can damage your credibility and reputation.

Think about it this way. Would you want to work with the lady who called the cops on a black family having a barbecue, or the lawyer who went on a racist rant and threatened to call ICE in a restaurant in New York, or any number of other people who've gone viral for being terrible humans? Even when you think you're out of the public eye, one bad day can ruin your reputation as a leader.

I can't overstate the importance of making sure everything you say or do supports a positive image of your brand. Give your followers every reason to support you and make sure to avoid giving your detractors anything to work with. There will always be people trying to tear you down; do not give them any leverage or ammunition to paint a negative picture of you when there is not one. You must be very intentional about everything you say and do to avoid giving fuel to people who want to take you down, and there are people who will do such a thing with no other reason than because they do not want to see you succeed.

Ensure your haters only have the flimsiest of excuses for not liking you. One wrong move could allow your haters the opportunity to drag you through the mud so much that even your greatest supporters are forced to separate themselves from you to salvage their own brand.

How do you build your brand?

As a leader, your brand is your verification. Potential followers, employers, and investors will choose whether or not to follow, hire, or invest in you based on your overall brand.

Start by asking those around you – friends, family, and your peers – what your brand looks like to the general public. Ask them to be completely honest with you. If they want you to grow, they should be willing to be honest with you about what others say about you, how you're being portrayed by people who do not fully know you, and what types of things you shouldn't be saying on social media.

It is likely you will get different answers from everyone that you ask. Most people behave differently around each group of people that they spend their time with. With that being said, you should hear common ideas, even though the exact comments may be diverse. If you don't, that is your first red flag. Regardless of what you say or do, everyone should be able to see the same values in you, no matter what location or surroundings that you find yourself in. This is a great starting point for building your brand.

You may laugh now, but as you get older, people will always remember previous versions of you. You never know what someone's last memory of you is. That's why you want to get insight from a lot of different people. Find out how older people, teachers, mentors, family members, younger people, church associates, your peers, and more feel about you. This will give you a clear idea of how your brand looks today and how you want it to look going forward. Think ahead to where you want your brand to be in the future. How do you want to be looked at 5 years from now? 10 years? 20 years?

Do you want the people at your job to think you are a hard worker but have a life outside of work? Or do you want them to see only what happens while in the office while keeping your personal life separate? If you're in college, do you want everyone to see your academic prowess, or just your service work, or just what you do at parties? Do you only want them to see one part of your lifestyle, or should they see that you're well-rounded? Part of branding yourself is who sees you, what they see, how they see you, and why you are showing them.

The difference between a good man and a great man is his visibility. You can't be a great leader if nobody sees it. Social media is a great tool for free visibility – but use it wisely. Any perceived negativity can put a damper on your brand. For example, if you let loose at a party, don't let your friends post drunk pictures of you on social media for the world to see. Your friends play a part in your branding as well, in more ways than one.

Perception is people's reality. If you do nine positive things and one negative thing, that one negative thing can change people's complete perception of you. Your reality is that you are a good person, but the person who focuses on that one thing they perceive as a negative will forever see you as a bad person.

Start building your brand early and be careful not to let anything blemish it. It takes a lot of hard work to build a brand and only one stupid mistake to shatter it. Be intentional when you choose what pictures, words, and quotes you put out into the world with your name attached to them.

Consistency is key. For example, what would you think if your boss was always rude and discourteous at work, but was the nicest person in the world at church? It would become increasingly hard to take that person serious, right? People should always know what to expect from you in every situation. You must be intentional about presenting a consistent image. Otherwise you run the risk of people picking and choosing which personalities they expect from you.

Know what type of leader you want to become. I'll discuss the different types of leaders in a later chapter and use that to build your brand. Radical leaders and religious leaders will need very different brands.

You need to think constantly about what type of person you want people to see you as and make sure everything you do in public upholds that image. Only do things you don't want the entire world to see when you are alone with people you trust not to leak things on their social media accounts.

Keep in mind that your life will be under a microscope and scrutinized at every turn. I can't overstate how important it is to manage every moment of your life in the public eye. This may sound like a lot of hard work, and it is, but the consequences of not maintaining a positive image can be catastrophic.

Building your brand

Who: Who is seeing you? Where are they seeing you? Are you a different person at church, at work, at the club, walking down the street, driving in your car, and at school? Is your brand the same in front of everyone? Are you going places where nobody you know might see you acting in a way that's contrary to your brand? You have control over who sees what in your life. With that being said, people will notice you without you even knowing. This means that your brand must be a genuine representation of yourself.

You must decide who you want to be. People will always talk about you without you knowing. Only you have control over what they say. It's very hard, but when you decide to become a leader, your life will be placed under a microscope. Be sure to do the right thing when you think nobody is watching because somebody is always watching.

What: What do people see when they look at you? What do you want people to think about you? That you're well-spoken, that you're wealthy, that you're level-headed? What is your goal for what you want people to think when they see you?

You control the narrative of your life, so take care about what you allow to be seen. There are certain things that you can no longer do because, as a leader, you are now seen as a role model, and in some cases, even a public figure. This doesn't mean you can't do anything that isn't strictly professional; it just means be careful about what you allow the world to see.

This relates directly to your "how." How you want people to see you will reflect directly on what you say and do.

How: What platforms are you being seen on? How should you conduct yourself on each of these platforms?

Social media:

It's important to get others' opinions of how you look on social media. If you have a bad image, then you must change it immediately. First, you need to consider who you want people to see, what you can say or do on your social media platform to back that up, and how you should change your social media platform going forward.

People can now see you with a wider lens. You have less control over what people see because your pictures and statements can be shared with people you don't know without your control. When used correctly, social media can be the greatest branding tool possible. Since millions of people are on each social media site worldwide, you can put out messages to be viewed by the masses. You must take full advantage of this opportunity. Put forth your best self on each social media tool and build a positive name for yourself.

If you need to change your brand, it's not necessary to create a new page, but you should completely delete all prior tweets, pictures, and messages. I recommend changing your profile picture and your "@ name." This will allow you to keep all your followers but push a new brand and a new message. It may take a while, but it will be worth it in the end.

Public: Public places include churches, schools, and social gatherings. These platforms are more intimate and give you more control of how you're viewed. Here, you can talk to people and verbally pass along your message. Keep in mind that people here will also notice you without you knowing. What makes it hard is that they see you more, and anything can be misconstrued or taken out of context. You must put forward a more consistent effort to maintain your brand in these locations.

Why: Why do you do the things you do? Do you make an effort to be the center of attention so that people see you as important, or is it because you want your brand to be seen by everyone? Do you dress up everywhere you go because you want people to see you as professional or classy? Do you drive a fancy car because you want people to think you have money? What are people noticing?

There are things you do because you have subconscious intentions. You must have pure intentions for each action you make. Knowing the reasons behind your actions and controlling them will give you more power over the impact of your brand.

Appearance

What do people see when they see you? How do you want to carry yourself? What's the first impression you want people to have before you even say "hello"? Think about how your choice of appearance may be perceived. Does it support your image?

Clothes: Are you always dressed up, always casual (street clothes), or do you prefer the care-free look?

Personal style: Do you always keep a clean cut? Do you go with a natural look and just let it flow?

Hygiene: People notice your personal hygiene. The way people perceive the way you carry yourself goes a long way. I personally always take a stance for professionalism; however, it is all a personal preference. Be warned, though, you will be judged accordingly.

Communication

How well do you communicate with strangers? Are you talkative or more reserved? Do you only talk to people you know, or do you work the room? Are you a great public speaker? How is your grammar? How is your body language – can people see you carrying your emotions on your sleeve? Note: this is a bad trait to have because your words will become less important if others are focused on your emotions instead of your words.

Body language is very powerful. It's important to gain control of your body language so that it can pass the message that you want people to see, regardless of how you truly feel. How well you communicate can have a significant impact.

Gravitas

Gravitas is composed of how you act and is deeply rooted in your character traits. Are you charismatic, honest, reliable, authentic? Do you show integrity and perseverance? These are some of the most important characteristics of a good leader. People can see these things through your actions or even in conversation. Take special care to develop these traits.

The people who you are seen with are also important. I'm sure you 've heard the phrase, "guilty by association." This works both ways, good and bad. Being associated with negative people can negatively impact the way that people perceive you. Being around people with positive reputations will go a long way in building your own reputation.

By no means is this fair, but it's a fact and must be treated as such. This doesn't automatically mean that it's necessary for you to change your friend group, however, you have been made aware and should move accordingly. Your character may be tested.

Your brand is directly correlated to your character as a person. People can see right through you and will notice if what you're displaying is authentic or just a facade. Why put on a fake front when you can just be the person that you display? This may mean working to build the character traits of honesty, integrity, perseverance, courage, etc. It will only take a little practice, and you will be positively rewarded for it in the end.

Right or wrong, you're going to be judged by the company you keep. Are you going to let this determine whether or not you hang out with your friends if the perception about them doesn't fit your brand? If you're seen around negative people, you may need to choose between distancing yourself from those people or taking it upon yourself to help change that other person's brand and image.

You must publicly support those around you

People will remember and reciprocate the support that you give. If people see that you are not supporting those in your own circle, then why would they want to support you? Every action that you make, intentionally or unintentionally, is being judged by your peers, so be careful of what messages you send. The way you treat those closest to you will be some-one's first indication of what they can expect from you.

You can only control your future by being cognizant of how people see you. Be intentional about how you carry yourself, who's around you, and everything you do. There is always somebody watching you.

The support component is so key because people will begin to notice what the support from those around you looks like as well. If you have an event, and no one from your team is present, then people will begin to wonder why that is and create their own reasons as to why. The question then becomes, "If the closest people to you do not support you, what is going on behind the scenes? Is this something that I would want to be a part of?"

Things people should never see you do

There are certain things people should never see you do. These are negative to your brand and should always be kept in private.

- Being drunk in public
- Arguing or fighting, whether it's verbally or physically
- Relationship disputes
- Being belligerent

What if I need to rebuild my brand?

Inconsistency is the quickest way to ruin a brand. The people in your support system should notice when things begin to go astray or let you know when it's time for a change.

If you need to start over, make sure everything across every platform of your brand is stripped, and you learn from your past mistakes.

Sometimes as you change, your brand must change, too. Maybe you posted some wild pictures on your social media as a teenager, but now that you're a young adult, you need to start rebuilding to show a more mature brand.

Become a new person. Any negative things attached to your old brand can still follow you unless you consistently behave differently. The definition of insanity is doing the same thing over and over again while expecting different results. You need to change your behavior to change your results. Make it clear that you are not the same person that you used to be.

It takes very little to tear a public image down and a whole lot of work to build one up. Be mindful of everything you do to avoid accidentally destroying your brand. Know that rebuilding a brand is very difficult because there will always be people who will remember the old you and try to use it to bring you down again or attempt to keep you down.

Your brand is about what people see, not so much of what you say. Make sure you're walking the walk and not just talking the talk. You can talk until you're blue in the face, but it won't do any good if your actions aren't backing up what you're saying.

Your brand should speak for itself when you walk in the room. You shouldn't have to constantly remind people of your accomplishments or tell them how good you are doing. If you build your brand the right way, then people will have already seen everything that you have done and may or may not speak on it to you. You know how well you are doing when people can speak to your accomplishments without you having to bring them up.

Do not tarnish a well-developed brand with hubris (having too much pride). Make it a point not to see yourself as too high to fall. Being brash and thinking too highly of yourself will be your downfall. You should never let cockiness taint your reputation. You worked hard for the things in your life, but you still need to remain humble.

Remember what your mother always told you, "Think before you speak." Be sure that you think about everything that you say or the actions that you make. You won't always receive a do-over.

CHAPTER 7

GOING GLOBAL

"The Boy Scouts live by a creed: 'leave no trace.' As leaders, I strive to leave a positive trace."[14]

Why is travel important for becoming a global leader?

For multiple reasons, it is an absolute must that you see the world. You shouldn't stifle yourself and your experience by not going out and seeing what the rest of the world has to offer. Seeing how other cultures live can be life-changing in regards to your personal point of view. You can learn how you have been taking the things you already have for granted as well as find a way to add new things to your life that you have previously only seen or read about.

Every country's government works differently. There is something to be said about someone who is open to using the things that work well with other leaders and using them in his or her own life. If you've only experienced democracy, you won't be able to appreciate the positive and negative qualities of it if you haven't seen how other governing styles work (or don't work, for that matter) in other parts of the world.

Growth is key, and you should look to grow your following globally. If major companies do it, then why wouldn't you want to do it?

The more you have seen and done, the more valuable your opinion becomes. If you have the same skills as somebody else, travel experience can add more value to your brand because you've seen and done things that not everyone has been able to, talked to people they've never met, and been to places they've only seen pictures of. It's crucial to add value to your brand whenever possible, and travel is a great way to do that.

You don't want to become stagnant as a person. Travel will help you push those boundaries to grow and learn in ways you can't even imagine. You should always aim to be the best possible version of yourself, and the growth you can experience through travel is irreplaceable. No one wants to get trapped being stuck in one way of thinking for the rest of their lives. Seeing new things, experiencing other cultures, learning new languages, and seeing how other civilizations have been able to flourish or flounder can expand the ways you think about life and give you new ideas and experiences to draw from as you grow as a leader. The more flexibility you have in your thinking, the more value you bring to the table.

The more things you've seen and done, the more it will open you up to new ideas. As you begin to develop plans and ideas, you will undoubtedly have more knowledge to draw from as well as have more experiences to have learned from. By way of experience, there will now be an entirely new group of people you will be able to relate to as well as communicate with. As new doors and opportunities begin to open for you, take advantage of the understanding you have from other parts of the world and make those unique experiences pave the way for innovation of concepts in your life.

Travel allows you to see outside your own neighborhood and get a glimpse of people who live differently than you. As a leader, it's important to be able to connect with all sorts of different people, and roaming the world is the best way to meet new people who live completely different lives and, on the surface, seem very different from you. Below the surface, however, they usually tend to be more similar to you than you would guess. You will never be able to learn that until you get out of your comfort zone and try something new.

Ignorance is not bliss. Living in a global society, the transfer of information can be done at the speed of light. However, many people seem to be comfortable with not moving any farther than their computer and miss out on the relationships and sharing of knowledge that can come from connecting with people. Use all of this information and go into new opportunities prepared with basic knowledge of the culture, language, and tradition of the type of people you will be encountering, and you will find that citizens in other countries have similar likes and interests as you. Don't hinder yourself by avoiding new experiences because you were afraid to learn for yourself, and instead, you just complacently read about it.

People, cultures, and governments do things differently in every corner of the globe. Seeing these differences first-hand will give you insight into how and why certain things happen the way they do. We get so used to seeing news on television and take the opinion or point of view of the source we learned it from. By doing so, we take away the chance to develop our own opinions because we only know what we're being told. The process of forming your own opinions comes from having the background knowledge to support your claim. The only way to gain that background knowledge is to feel another culture for yourself; otherwise, you will always see their actions and responses from a single point of view or someone else's agenda.

Make a list of places you want to go. List all of the countries that you want to see; include every adventure, moment, or attraction that you've always wanted to experience in person. Then, set a specific plan for how you are going to make this trip happen. Begin setting money aside, start looking into hotels and flight information, even start trying to learn pieces of the language like popular phrases. The more you start planning for it, the more serious or realistic this trip starts to become to you. Stop allowing travel to be stuck in a dead end dream. Make an effort to take the steps necessary to put yourself in the position to go where you want to go. You only live one life; do not miss out on all the beauty that the world has to offer because you held yourself back. Make it happen. Start saving money now. Travel is a mind over matter issue. Think to yourself that you will do whatever it takes to travel. Don't let life pass you by.

Serving in a mission capacity overseas is a great way to kill two birds with one stone. You get the opportunity to help people and to see beautiful scenery. You can go into countries that need assistance (whether from a natural disaster or a terribly-run government) and offer your aid as an individual and as a team. It is common to believe that serving others in need is life-changing to those being served, but the truth is, it is much more life-changing to the ones who serve. Be sure when you are serving other that you are doing more good than harm. Sometimes giving people what you think they need may be offensive, an intrusion on their livelihood, or even giving them a feeling of inferiority that they did not previously experience. The best rule of thumb is to be sure you saturate your service in LOVE.

The great thing about involving yourself in service activities in other countries is that you receive an authentic cultural experience. There is a difference between travelling to vacation areas of a country and travelling into the alley ways and countryside. Resorts are definitely beautiful and accommodating, but they do not let you experience how the natives who work there live on a daily basis.

How do you take your leadership skills from country to country?

Decide before you travel, even on vacations, what you think you want to learn. You will learn more than you expect and many surprising things along the way, but setting out to learn something specific will help you get the most out of your trip.

Serve a purpose. If you are a connector, seek out connections overseas. If you're a teacher, find opportunities to teach wherever you travel, despite any language barriers you may come across.

Once you learn how to get around language, culture, and other barriers as you travel the world, you will be able to take those experiences back home and find it easier to overcome barriers with people who are similar to and different than you. If you can survive these barriers, then nothing at home will be able to get in your way.

Using mission trips to practice leadership while traveling

Mission trips are a very specific way to travel with intent. They are about service to a community, learning more about the indigenous people, getting out of your comfort zone, learning humility, and putting someone else's happiness before your own. A book could never do this experience justice. Serving through mission work will give you an experience that puts your strength to the test. I'm not talking about your muscles but your emotional strength and your strength of character. You will be placed in situations where you have to put another person before yourself, and it will test your heart.

Service is important to becoming a leader, so mission trips are a great way to get that exposure and expand your range of service and concern. You can have all the same fun of a vacation while also being able to help people. What can be better than that? For some, finding opportunities with mission trips may be the way you get out of the country for the first time. I never used my passport until I was invited on my first mission trip in 2014 to Haiti. It was a life-changing experience to serve a country that had been ravaged by a hurricane just years earlier.

Mission work overseas will be one of the most humbling things you will ever experience.

My first mission trip

I took my first mission trip, to Haiti, the summer going into my senior year of high school. It was just a few years after the 2010 earthquake that devastated the small country, and the community was still struggling.

My initial thought was to go help these individuals that everyone deemed poor. I felt that there was a lot I could teach them because of the privilege I had attained in the United States. Little did I know that the people of Haiti would prove me wrong, and instead, I would learn and gain more than I could have ever imagined from them.

When people think about Haitians, they think of them as part of a third world country, the poorest in the western hemisphere. What people fail to realize is that, although they may be living in third world conditions, they have first world personalities.

While in Haiti, we saw things I wasn't prepared for. An orphanage of 30 children stands out the most. The children lived in an environment where there was no roof nor a working door; it was just a hole in the wall which we walked through. Everyone from the children to the caretaker slept in a small cell where there were only a few beds that they all shared. *The only meal available to them was a bowl of rice every day, donated from* Feed the Hungry. The area in which they played consisted of a nearly flat soccer ball and soccer goals created with what remained from the fence that once stood in its place and whatever rope they could find to suffice for a net. Each child that I encountered was marked with tremendous amounts of pain and suffering, yet they still found a way to smile through it all.

There are still two images that continue to resonate in my mind. A small boy, no older than 7 and never knowing his parents, sat in front of me barefoot. As a foot-washer, I washed his feet, rubbed lotion on them, and gave him a brand new pair of shoes. After he put both feet into his brand-new pair of shoes, he jumped out of the chair and embraced me in his small arms. At the time, I could not even fathom the emotion that he must have been going through. As we continued to communicate, he expressed to me about how this was his first time receiving a gift and that he may never see another.

The next orphan came and sat in front of me. Immediately, I noticed that he was missing an arm. Through our interpreter, I found out that he lost his left arm in the earthquake. Having been trapped under rubble for a number of days, he felt lucky just to be able to survive. His parents were left under the rubble as rescue teams, very well-intentioned but understaffed, could not save them. As I washed his feet, I was almost brought to tears when I heard his story.

Handicapped and homeless, I expected him to be angry and bitter, as I can almost guarantee that I would have been at the age of no older than 10. However, he was none of the sort. In fact, he giggled as I rubbed lotion through his toes the same as many of us had done as infants. "We are lucky for every new day that we see and should enjoy every moment of it," he conveyed. As I presented him with a new pair of shoes, he smiled ear to ear. In most cases, after we gave them a new pair of shoes, we would discard their old pair if it was too worn out. However, this young man was adamant about returning to his meal with the other children with his old shoes in hand.

A country of people who had every reason to hate the world after a disaster that was no fault of their own and completely obliterated the lives that they remembered from just years ago, were some of the most upbeat and fun-loving people that I had met in my short stint on Earth. I will never forget the immense weight that I felt lift off of my heart after leaving that orphanage. In this lifetime, we are met with few opportunities to have life-altering experiences, so be sure to make the best of those opportunities when the time arises. These opportunities aren't always meant to change someone else's life, but to change your own. Find an experience that will help you grace every new person that you encounter with your new-found prowess of delivering joy.

*It turns out that I was wrong about Haiti. She helped me more than I could have ever even conceived to benefit her. Before I arrived, I had half-*expected this luxurious hotel with wi-fi and easily accessible connection to the world outside of us. However, that was not the case at all. Since I couldn't connect with anyone back home, I decided to turn my phone off for the duration of the trip. This forced me to sit down and have face-to-face interactions. My roommate and I sat and talked for hours every night about life and its meanings. We discussed our differences in religion as well as our varying methods of aiding the people around us.

The last night in Haiti, we began our usual group discussion on how the day went and how everyone felt after the day's adventures. We talked about the major revelations that everyone expected us to return home with, but we realized that it isn't a change in person, but a change in mindset we would soon return with. That night, we set a goal as individuals and as a larger group that we would hold each other to. From that point on, when we came in contact with new individuals, we wanted people to see us as first-world not on the outside, but on the inside.

How do I make my impact felt?

John Martin, CEO of the Young Black Leadership Alliance and founder of the Young Black Male (YBM) Leadership Alliance said: "The Boy Scouts live by a creed: 'leave no trace.' As leaders, I strive to leave a positive trace."[14]

When you leave an area, the people should feel better than they did before you arrived. People should remember what you did while you were there, even after you've left. The impact you have on a person will not be the actions you took or the things that you did for them, but what memories and messages they leave with when you're no longer around. Leave that person saying, "They taught me something; they changed this part of my life for the better." If you can change somebody's life for the better, they will follow you forever, because they know that you have a genuine agenda in regards to them.

On this journey called life, everyone hopes to leave an impact that others can remember them for. That impact won't be left by the number of cars that you have, the size of the home you live in, or the amount of money you acquire. Your impact will be measured by the number of people that you touch along the way. The most universal way to get to know someone is over a meal. The act of communion is by far the most intimate setting to engulf yourself in one's culture. Deep conversation over a good meal will leave a lifelong impact on new friends.

CHAPTER 8

BEING A LEADER

"There are three types of people in the world: those who make it happen, those who watch it happen, and those for whom things happen because of who you are."[15]

You don't have to be "the leader" to be "a leader"

When it comes to leadership, everyone feels that if they're not the person making all the decisions, then they're not a leader. That couldn't be any farther from the truth.

If you look at successful leaders, the ones whose faces will always be remembered, they couldn't have done anything without the people behind them helping along the way. It may not always fall in place for you to be front and center, but if you genuinely care about what you're doing, then that shouldn't even matter. Often, your responsibility will be to assist in the growth of someone else, and you will have to be able to accept your role as the situation unfolds. One's humility will be tested when he or she doesn't receive the role or responsibility that they want, but they still put the good of the movement before their own personal agenda.

One major problem in our society is that everybody wants to be THE leader. Many humans tend to want their name to go up in bright lights and big letters. It has become increasingly obvious that people would rather not bring a larger group together to fulfill the same mission if they will not be the person in supreme control. Furthermore, it is imperative to think small and build up. Remember, Rome wasn't built in a day, but brick by brick.

Touch the people that are around you first. Give them your full attention and maximum effort. Everybody wants to change the world, but they often forget to change their inner community. If you could develop every city one at a time, then would the state not be better developed? If you could improve each state one by one, then would the country not end up better developed? Become laser focused on the "greater good".

Don't be afraid to think small or develop small goals en route to your larger mission. Some leaders stay small in com- parison to others, and that is perfectly fine. Help the people you're the most passionate about. Do the best work you can, whether that's in your neighborhood, your school, or even your city. As a matter of fact, start in your own home. Don't fall into the trap of thinking too big and forgetting about the little details. When it is time for you to move on to something bigger, then you will know. You must simply be ready for the opportunity when it reveals itself.

For a major corporation to run effectively for a long period of time, there are various levels of leadership that make it possible to function. You have a CEO who communicates information to the members on his executive board, their CFOs and COOs. Then, the same message must be expressed to the managers, who then, in turn, decipher and communicate that message to the rest of the employees. Why would your team be set up any differently?

I say all of that to emphasize that for a team to run, there needs to be leaders at every level, and each leader must be comfortable in his or her role and perform to the best of their ability. Sometimes it is necessary that you lead from the background. We all have to find our role and niche on the team and do it to the fullest of our capabilities.

Mistakes and shortcomings get bigger the higher you get, so build slowly and perfect your craft. So many people begin to grow faster than they anticipate and don't get the chance to learn as they grow. Then, all of a sudden, something goes wrong, and they find themselves stuck trying to figure out where they went wrong. But now you have all these people looking to you for answers, and if you can't answer their questions, they begin to lose faith in you.

So don't be in a rush to grow; build the right way, and the rest will surely fall into place. Focus on your passion; you may not change the world directly, but if you can change your community, that can lead to a regional change, which can inspire a nationwide change, and it only goes up from there. Focusing on being a leader, even in a small capacity, can still leave a ripple effect that can change the entire world once you're gone. You can change the world by changing one community at a time.

Without passion, you will always be unhappy, looking outside your bubble. It's important to enjoy each moment while still focusing on the big picture.

What makes a good leader?

A good leader leads by example. It can't be a case of "Do as I say, not as I do." You must constantly be the change you want to see. Those who follow you will imitate your actions. You will find yourself having to constantly motivate your team and build morale. They will look to you, especially when they lose momentum or times get hard. Success comes with setbacks. When those setbacks hit, your character as a leader will show. When times get tough, will you rise to the occasion or fold under pressure?

With that being said, you must translate that character to your team. If you have a team of high-character members, then nothing will be able to hold you back. 20% of the people generally do 80% of the work, so you must be willing to put in the work to build something you can be proud of. Becoming a leader isn't easy. Not everyone will put in the same quality of work; sometimes, you just have to do something yourself.

Those who follow you should never doubt the process of whatever task you are looking to complete. You will also have to keep their minds stimulated on the job at hand. Many people will leave or fall off if there isn't always something to be done or it seems like the tasks always appear to be completed quickly or without much effort. This doesn't have to always come in the form of more work. This could easily be challenging them to come up with new ideas or to even have them work on a task that will overwhelm you. Make them feel like they're appreciated and that their talents are being utilized effectively.

Everyone looks to you for guidance as a leader, especially through times of adversity. You have to be the person to sit down and talk people through tough times. You must lead by example through demonstrating patience, understanding and applying experience and wisdom.

You may have to give some things up. Knowing that others will follow your example, you may need to give up certain vices that you don't want your followers to pick up. For example, trying to encourage kids to stay away from drugs and alcohol while having a cigarette dangling from your mouth, may not be the best way to send an impactful message. You have to be more careful about what you're seen saying and doing.

It will be inevitable that you become a good public speaker. After all, your great idea means nothing if you're unable to communicate your point across to those who need to hear it. Since public speaking is the most common fear in the world, organizations such as Toastmasters International can help you practice your speaking skills in a friendly, non-threatening environment. If you're still in school, consider joining the debate team or working closely with a teacher that can help build that significant quality in you.

Many people only speak about humility in relation to not being cocky or self-centered. However, one must also take into account the humility necessary to listen to others' ideas. The greatest leaders know how to empower on their team to be in charge of certain tasks. Being able to delegate duties is an under-rated skill that must be developed in order to perform many tasks at one time. Not only because you can't do it all yourself, but because sometimes someone else may have a better idea or concept than you. You should not only embrace this idea, but encourage and teach it.

It's important to remain consistent. If you do something consistently enough for long enough, you will get the compound impact you desire. If you can build people's faith in you, they will never leave. BE WARNED, if you build false hope, it will all backfire before your eyes and ruin your brand.

Yes, new tasks or random events will pop up on your agenda, but don't allow these things to take you out of your normal routine. Make consistent practices a part of your schedule, but be flexible. It will be beneficial to have meetings set up weekly and either a newsletter or a memo to be released monthly. This allows you to have a stream of information coming out on a regular basis and eliminates the chance of random tasks and information surprising those who need it. As the leader, your team should always know what they're getting out of you.

You have to be consistent as you work and grow. If people see you all over the place and trying to multitask, how will you be able to tell your team to focus on one task at a time? Most people do what they see, not what they are told.

Confidence may be the most important trait to have. When you exude confidence, people will automatically flock to you. If you make a statement with confidence, people will believe it. The aura of confidence can be felt by most people. No matter how rough it may get, there will be hard times, but your confidence must never waver. If people see you losing confidence, then they will lose confidence as well. You must set a precedent for those around you.

If your confidence wavers, the faith of your team members will surely waver. Even if things are bad, you need to put on a brave face. It's all about building faith. If people lose faith in you, nobody will listen to what you say. If a body of people do not have faith in what they're doing, nothing will work.

The flip side to having confidence is backing it up by being completely competent in what you speak about. You don't want to lead people in the wrong direction because you don't know what you're talking about. People can see through someone who constantly doesn't have the correct information.

The power of using "we" over "I" can't be overstated. You need to engage your team and build morale. Just the inclusion of the team in your conversations with them will make them feel like everything being done will be for the good of them as well. Always thinking of them before you make decisions will go a long way to them being fully invested. As you make an effort to bring the team together, they will notice and reciprocate the effort back to you through their work.

You must speak your mind with the team. The team should always be on the same page. If there is something that you don't like, talk about it. When they do something good, speak on it. Communication is key. If you wait to speak up, an unwanted habit may be created that you will never be able to stop. You want to nip that behavior in the bud. Talk about positives and congratulate your team, no matter how small of a success you've had as a team. Always build the confidence of your team. You shouldn't be the only person on your team who knows how you want things done. Everybody should know the next steps. Be sure the each individual member of the team is being shown appreciation for the value they provide.

Be sure to keep emotions separate from the good of the team. Do not allow short-term feelings to derail long-term goals. This must be instilled in the team because there will be times when someone is having a bad day, or team members don't agree with one another, and they will have to put those feelings aside for the time being so the team can prosper.

However, depending on what is going on, you should speak with them outside of the group and see what you can offer to help, whether it be advice or just lending a listening ear. Just do not allow temporary emotions to interfere with long-term success.

Faith is key. If everyone has faith in what's going on, then they will always be engaged and never leave. You have to make sure the team believes in what you are doing. Having faith will mean the difference in them just going through the motions and doing the bare minimum, and them going above and beyond for you. They will cease to follow you if they can no longer see the same vision they bought into.

Because faith is so important, be sure to generate it right away. Don't lead somebody down the wrong path. So much about being a leader is about your character. People are going to talk, and word will spread. Your brand can be torn down by negative experiences. If people see you can't be trusted with people close to you, nobody else will trust you.

The best team learns from a multitude of voices, so you should not be the only one feeding into them, nor should you get mad when someone else does. Everyone should be on the same page. You may need other leaders to step in, or you may even need to bring in somebody who isn't on your team to come in to elaborate and repeat what you said. For example, your mom can tell you to do something 100 times, but it only clicks when you hear it from your teacher instead. Sometimes things click when they come from another voice.

Don't let them be codependent on you, because if you miss a day, then the whole team misses a day.

You will need to change your leadership style as you grow. As I discuss the different styles of leaders, you will see that some styles, such as the participative leader, will work better with small organizations, while other leadership styles will work better in larger organizations. While you will typically use one leadership style more than the others, you should be familiar with all the styles and use them as needed, depending on the situation.

Be flexible about changing your leadership style based on the composition of your team. Different people need to be led in different ways. Being able to lead people in a hundred different ways will benefit you and the people choosing to follow you. This is where being charismatic comes into play. Having a compelling charm about yourself is a quality that draws many people and their loyalty to you. Everyone leads in different ways. Observe other leaders and take pieces of their leadership style that you admire to work into your leadership style. People will be more likely to follow somebody who is charismatic and outgoing rather than shy and introverted.

You shouldn't be the only leader that your team hears. Think back to a time when you were young and still living under your parents' roof. There would be certain times that your parents repeatedly attempted to teach you an important lesson. Since they were always telling you the same thing, you started tuning them out or not hearing it with the utmost importance. Yet, someone else could tell you the same thing, and it would sink in automatically. That's how it is in a position of leadership sometimes. Good leaders make themselves willing and able to empower other leaders on their team or place their team in the hands of other mentors.

Bring in other leaders that the members on your team respect and have them reiterate some of the points that you've made. Let your message be delivered by many voices, multiple times and multiple ways. Studies show that a human needs to hear or do something at least 28 times for it to be completely committed to one's memory. So the more that you can reinforce key concepts to your team, the better off you all will be in the long run.

Find your identity as a leader

Your leadership identity differs from your leadership style. Your identity requires deeper thought and is the only way you can purposefully grow. It's important to have some parts of each leadership style embedded into your leadership identity, despite whichever seems to become your dominant style. Your style must evolve based on the size, culture, and demographics of your following. It's easier to be participative with smaller groups than larger ones, and it's easier to be delegative in a larger group. As you find the culture of your team, you will begin to notice the way they react to certain decisions, events and obstacles, as well as the manner in which they behave based off of certain actions. Adjust accordingly and tailor yourself to fit the group around you, not the other way around.

Above all, be sure to show recognition to those around you. It doesn't always have to be a large celebration or something elaborate, but be sure to show the team that you appreciate them and that you notice all of their hard work. By doing so, they will always feel that they can do anything, and that is the atmosphere that you want to construct around you.

Different leadership styles

In 1939, psychologist Kurt Lewin led a group of researchers in identifying different styles of leadership. This is what his team concluded.

#1 - Authoritarian/Autocratic With this style of leadership, you make all the decisions with little to no input from others. You need to provide clear expectations about what you want to be done and when and how to do it. This style can be more efficient in very large organizations, but those under you will tend to be less creative in their decision-making, and it can create a hostile environment where the followers rebel against their leader.

#2 – Participative/Democratic This has been shown to be the most effective style of leadership in most situations. Democratic leaders let the others in their group help with the decision-making process, although they retain the final say. Followers feel more included and valued and tend to produce higher-quality and more creative results. Participative leadership can lead to decreased productivity in certain situations.

#3 – Delegative/Laissez-faire In delegative leadership, the leader leaves nearly all decision-making to those under them. It can be useful when you need to defer to experts, but overall, a lack of guidance can lead to a lack of motivation and decreased personal responsibility.

What qualities make powerful leaders so influential?

#1 – Great speaking ability. The best leaders in history were known for their resonating speeches. Their words were clear, concise, compelling and to the point. After hearing Dr. King, you almost had no choice but to believe in what he was saying. The power of his presence on stage was only superseded by the words and tone that he used to touch people's hearts and stimulate their minds.

#2 – Relatability. Great leaders seem like they could be your friend in the right circumstances. You feel that they understand you in a way that many others don't. As President Obama ran for office, every step of the way, he and his family exuded a feeling of being at home. It always seemed that as he spoke, whatever he was saying would help me in the long run.

#3 – Charisma. Charisma is a type of irresistible charm that can grab a listener's attention and persuade them to want what you want or unite for a common cause. Take a look at John F. Kennedy. Everywhere he went, a procession of devoted admirers and enthusiasts were always sure to follow.

#4 – Likable personality. Napoleon made up for his lack of size and stature with his ability to befriend anyone that he came into contact with. There is something to be said about a man who could cultivate the love of an entire country and become the leader without an ounce of royal blood.

CHAPTER 9

NETWORKING

"Performance + Relationships = Advancement."[16]

The goal of networking

The goal of networking is to build your chance at opportunity through the people that you are connected with. The more people that you have a relationship with, the more opportunities that you open yourself to receive. You never know what someone can do for you or what opportunities may come just from being around any given person.

The more people you have around you, the more opportunities you have. You have to network organically and genuinely. It should be a relationship where both parties benefit. The premise is that someone would rather give an opportunity to someone that they know very well and could vouch for rather than a complete stranger, which is why it is imperative to build strong and lasting relationships. You never know when an opportunity may come your way, so you must maintain all of these relationships. That is why it is a good practice for these relationships to be genuine, so you can reap the benefits of holding on to them.

As you network, you must put yourself in a position to meet people who have opportunities that you are seeking. If you want to build your network in the medical field, then you should be where physicians spend their time. If you want to meet more educators, then spend your time where educators spend theirs. You must strategically place yourself in positions to meet who you want. Do not leave it up to chance.

The best way to put yourself in a good position to network is to research events held for the group you're looking for. If you want to meet an executive at Bank of America, then you should find a way to go to their annual gala or community service events. If you're a teacher and want to meet more principals, go to the conferences for administrators.

The goal is to put yourself in the right place at the right time. Sometimes it may take a little research, but if you really want to build your network, then that is time well spent. We live in a world where it isn't about what you know but who you know. So don't do yourself a disservice by attempting to rely on what you know.

How well you do your job is only part of the equation for advancement. The other key component is the relationships that you can leverage. Knowing someone who is sitting in the room as they decide who gets the promotion will go a long way to helping you get into the position that you want. You want people to vouch for your character and your work ethic, which makes you stand out as a candidate, because no one is in the business of taking risks on people that they know nothing about.

Either keep in contact or keep a directory of the people that you network with. You never know when you may need them. Better yet, you never know when they could offer you something new. Often people in high positions have the power to give opportunities that you may not be able to find otherwise. Leverage that as you look to grow personally and as a leader. In addition to the opportunity that they could provide to you, each person that you come into contact with has a wealth of knowledge that you can learn from. Don't discredit anyone's position, because you never know who could send something your way that changes your life.

Most importantly, don't be afraid to ask. Too many people miss out on opportunities because they were too afraid to ask for what they wanted, and an opportunity just passed them by. If someone is willing to help you, don't let your pride get in the way of a blessing. If someone has invested enough time into you to sit down and have a conversation, then they are surely open enough with you to want to help.

Invite these people out to your events and be sure to go to theirs. Use this time to get to know each other better and to find other ways that you can benefit each other. Having a mutually beneficial relationship is a recipe for success. For those of you who think you may have nothing to benefit someone who "has more than you," just pure knowledge through conversation and genuineness is enough for most people. There are people who are wired to help others through mentoring or providing opportunities.

Who to network with

Ideally, your goal should be to find people who are in a position that you would like to attain. Maybe you're still in college and want to be a doctor, so you should be networking with doctors. If you have an entry-level position, then attempt to network with the people above you: managers, vice presidents, executives, and anyone else you see that could potentially help you attain a better position. Take the information and experience that they have and make it fit your situation. Learning from other people's mistakes and triumphs will surely expedite your success. Ask questions like: How did you get to the position you are in now? Do you enjoy your position? If you had an opportunity to do it over again, what would you do differently? Do you have any other advice that may be helpful? Who else do you think I should talk to?

Never burn bridges. Strive to create positive networking experiences and leave everyone with a favorable impression. You never know when you may see them again. More importantly, you never know when you could utilize them in the future. People talk, so burning a bridge could cause that person to give a bad review of you to somebody else who had thought about helping you. We live in a very small world, and word travels fast. Do not lose an opportunity because of bad manners, poor body language or some other unfavorable impression. Always be courteous and professional, even if the situation does not demand it. It will all pay off in the end.

Too often, people miss opportunities or feel like networking is not providing dividends. Be patient. Opportunities are not always presented in the short run. Do not cut ties just because you do not see an immediate payoff. It is possible that someone in your network could change jobs and present a new opportunity for you. It would help if you created an Excel spreadsheet on your computer to log everyone's name, number, email address, profession, the name of their company, and any other important notes (people love when you remember something personal). You may find yourself in a position to be able to provide an opportunity to someone else.

Diversify your networking tactics. Do not limit yourself to the places you go and the number of people you speak to. Cast a wide net into several waters. Although it is a good idea to network wherever you go, remember that the quality of a relationship means a lot more than the number of connections you have. Five great relationships will do you more good than 20 mediocre connections. Meeting the CEO of your company one time doesn't do as much for you as having a vice president in the company as a mentor.

Do not find yourself chasing titles just to be able to tell people that you've met them. Spend your time fostering the connections you have and use them to grow your network from the inside out. You would be surprised who someone could introduce you to. I personally have not worked any job that I had to submit an application or conduct interviews for. I've utilized my mentors and propelled myself forward by doing great work. Your network can get you in the door, but only your work ethic can keep you there.

Some of the people you meet will not result in long-lasting relationships. Some of these people will only be contacts, but that doesn't mean they can't be useful. Everyone you speak to can help you in the long run. Be open to opportunity. We all get offered opportunities, but most of us miss out on them because we have tunnel vision. We may be so focused on a particular goal that we miss a more lucrative one staring us in the face.

Networking is a 24/7 endeavor. Don't get caught taking days off. There is no substitute for a great network. Be on the lookout everywhere you go. Networking doesn't just happen at parties and in the office, it happens in the mall, at the auto shop, at a concert, on the subway and at a basketball game.

Following up with new contacts

A lot of people struggle with what to do after you've made a new contact. The most important rule is ALWAYS REACH OUT WITHIN 2-3 DAYS. Sending a follow-up email is key. It will set a precedent for that relationship by sending the message that you were honored to meet them and you look forward to adding value to each other's lives. If they don't email back, then depending on how important that relationship is, send another email to remind them.

Here are examples of templates you can use when calling or emailing new contacts to establish a relationship.

Follow-up Call (after meeting)

Greeting [Good Morning, Day, Afternoon, or Evening]

Pleasure speaking/meeting [Remind contact of where you met – Day, Event, or Location]

I gained/I learned [share what you specifically gained and/or learned from the event, experience, or conversation] – this puts them in "recall" of the interaction.

I wanted to follow-up to: [Move to action, with a timeline]

"I want to get on your calendar within the *next two weeks* for a quick cup of coffee…"

"I'm calling to get the contact info for…"

"I'm calling to remind you of…"

"You asked me to follow-up to do…"

Create Value for the action: Consider -

Does this action benefit them?

Why should they do this (action)?

How does this action help, or who does it benefit?

What are you asking them to do?

- Make a connection intro call
- Meet to share info
- Meet to mentor
- Come to an event

Thanks, and Close [show sincere gratitude]

Utilize this opportunity to add value to the relationship by giving a compliment or stroke their ego.

Close the call with a quick recap.

Follow-Up Email

Greetings: [Good Morning, Day, Afternoon, or Evening] Prefix and Last Name,

Intro: [Give a general one sentence soft start to the email]

"I hope things are going well…"

"I'm having an incredible day, and hope you are…"

"It's a great day here in Charlotte; I hope all is well with you…"

Reminder of Meeting [Establish re-connection by recalling day, event, or location of meeting]

"It was good to meet you at the event at the location on this day…"

"I enjoyed our conversation at event…"

Share something meaningful or impactful that you enjoyed that they said or you heard.

"It was great to find out that…"

"I was intrigued by…"

"It's amazing that…"

Move To Action: [state what you would like to happen next, with a timeline]:

- If you are asking to meet to *establish* a relationship, ask for a quick meet or cup of coffee.

"I'd like to get on your calendar within the next two weeks to have a quick meeting to..."

"I'd like to schedule a *quick 10-minute* call in the *next two days*, to speak about..."

Create Value for the action: Consider -

Does this action benefit them?

Why should they do this (action)?

How does this action help, or who does it benefit?

What are you asking them to do?

- Make a connection intro call
- Meet to share info
- Meet to mentor
- Come to an event

"I'm looking forward to..."

"I'm excited about ..."

"It's great to know that you..."

Salutation:

"Best Regards"

"Sincerely"

"Respectfully"

"All the Best"

E-signature

Name (First and Last)

Organization/Job Title

Phone #

Email

What should you talk about when you meet over the phone or in person? Discuss personal stories, goals, and plans. Never go into a meeting without wanting to learn something. If you are only looking to speak with them so that you can say you met them, you have already wasted both of your times. Write down a list of at least three to five questions that you would like to ask this person. If you can't come up with at least three questions, then this may not be the right person for you connect with.

The following are suggestions of what you should be looking to learn about: the path that helped them get to their current level of success, what characteristics and skills they have seen in people that have made others successful, and what you could be doing to help set a path to success in your current field of interest. If the first meeting goes well, then try to set up a follow-up meeting. A phone call would be a good way to keep them updated on your progress. Never leave these meetings without a goal or a task to be able to give them updates on.

How can you help them? Relationships must be mutually beneficial. You can't just contact somebody with the hope of getting something from them without giving anything in return.

Other great questions to ask your mentor:
What is the greatest lesson you ever learned?
What are you learning now?
How has failure shaped your life?
What have you read that I should read?

What have you done that I should do?

Where have you been that I should go?

Who do you know that I should know?

What are the things in your life that you value the most?

What are you most passionate about?

How can I add value to you?

How to ask for and give out business cards

As the conversation comes to a close and you decide that you would like to stay in contact with this person, you will want to request a business card from them. In doing so, you will now have access to their phone number and email address. Be sure, once they give you their card, that you clarify which is the best way to reach them: by email or by phone. Make a point to write down a way for you to remember them from this conversation; you will meet a lot of people and receive a lot of information, so do not put yourself in a situation where you forget who was who (that's one reason why it is important that you always carry a pen with you). Make sure you add all of their information to your Excel spreadsheet with all your connections on it. Reach out to them within two or three days and follow the template for emails and phone calls.

Don't be afraid to go up and talk to anyone; they are people just like you. People enjoy being asked for help, so let them help you. Just because somebody has a title doesn't make them any higher or lower than you. You need to transform connections into relationships by continuing to be genuine and treating everyone like regular people.

Everyone won't connect well with you; don't let that discourage you. The goal is to find quality relationships, not a bunch of bad ones. Sometimes it's just a numbers game. Of five people, maybe only three reach back out to you and only one becomes a mentor for you. The more people you meet, the more opportunities you will have.

Holding onto your connections

Once every few months, you should check in to see how the people in your network are doing. Reach out to people. If an opportunity is meant to come, it will. If you're genuine in your interactions with others, opportunities will be there. If you tear down bridges, you will never get there. You should invite people to see what you're doing and allow them to network with your team.

This is how you find your mentors. When you find someone that gives you a good vibe, get to know them. If you guys click, ask them to be your mentor. These relationships must be built genuinely and can't be forced.

The longer these relationships have time to develop, the closer you will become and the more opportunities that can be made abundant to you. There are mentors that I've had since I was a junior in high school who I'm just now tapping into almost 10 years. Don't miss out on something life-changing because you were lazy, impatient, or unprepared.

Merging networks

Your network should be introducing you to people in their networks and vice versa. Invite people to your events and begin attending theirs. Bring your team to meet them. If they share information, they may have somebody on their team you don't know either. Even if somebody can't do something for you directly, they might know somebody who can. The goal is to be able to help other people achieve their goals, so be sure to make a point to help connect them with people who can help. There is no award for keeping all of your connections to yourself.

Don't Burn Bridges

My cousin threw a cookout and invited the entire family and a few close friends. As we were eating, one of his friends walked into the backyard. Out of the corner of my eye, I saw that he had on a shirt with my university's name on it. Of course, I asked him about it, and he began to explain how he was an alumni and his son was about to graduate from there in a couple of months. Intrigued, I asked his son's name. To both of our surprises, I knew his son. Better than that, his son and I frequently hung out on campus throughout our tenure at North Carolina A&T State University. The gentleman proceeded to call to his wife and express to her what had just taken place outside.

While we had been outside talking, my mother and his wife were in the kitchen discussing their children and what they had been doing all summer. As my mother spoke about the experience I was currently having at my internship, the woman let my mother know that she just so happens to work at the same company I was interning for.

After the gentleman called to his wife and she came outside, she noticed that I looked familiar and asked where we knew each other. We began going down the list of places that we may have crossed paths and then it hit me. This was the woman who had interviewed me almost eight months prior for my current internship. Of course, everyone then wanted to know how well I interviewed and what I was like away from my parents. With excitement, the woman expressed how well my interview went and about how we talked about our personal lives, then the job. She enjoyed the conversation we had as we interviewed, and she exclaimed how great of a message she reported back to the hiring manager about me afterward.

The underlying message to this story is that it is crucial to never burn bridges. Look back to a previous chapter where we mention always leaving people with a good image of you. You never know when you may see people again, but you can control what they say about you when they do see you.

CHAPTER 10

DUPLICATION

"I measure success in terms of the contributions an individual makes to her fellow human beings."[17]

Leave a legacy

How do you want to be remembered when your time here on Earth has expired? Do you want people to remember you for the level of education that you attained? Or maybe by the amount of money you were able to acquire in your lifetime? Success isn't determined by the number of cars you own, the square footage of the house you live in, or how much money you were able to attain, but by the number of people that you were able to impact with the power of your words and actions.

As you commence your path to success, begin to think about what type of impact you would like to leave. Who do you want to feel that impact, or what group of people's lives do you intend to change for the better throughout your lifetime? As you start to answer this question, it will make the next step increasingly easy for you. Once you indicate who you want your impact to be felt by, you're ready to embark on the path to leaving a larger legacy than just yourself.

To leave your lasting legacy, your mission cannot end when you decide to stop or cannot do what you're doing anymore. You must invest in other people, developing them to be able to follow in your footsteps. It begins to resemble the trickle-down effect; everything that you teach them, they, in turn, teach to someone else. As those teachings continue to be passed down, your message starts to be introduced to people that you have yet to meet. That is how a man leaves a legacy that will be remembered for generations to come. As your legacy lives through the people you invested in, so do you. As long as your name lives, then the impact that you left will live with it.

Teach one to impact many

You won't be able to do what you're doing forever, so you should be prepping someone to continue the mission when you have done all that you can do. Often, you may just find something else that demands more of your attention and need someone to take charge over what you're currently working on. If the purpose of what you do is authentic, then the work will never be done or completed; it just keeps growing and either serving a larger group or a larger purpose.

Having said that, someone should always be ready to take control of the reins when you're ready to step down or move to something different. Furthermore, operations should never cease in the case that you are inactive for any reason. If you're not there because you miss a day or have to put your attention elsewhere, who will step up and keep business running as usual?

It is very difficult to attempt to do everything on your own; that is why it is imperative that you begin teaching other people how to do the things you do well. You don't have to instruct a large number of people on everything, because you should utilize the art of the trickle-down effect. When you teach two people something and they each teach two people the same thing, now you have just taught six people the same lesson while only having to personally speak with two of them. Now, all of them may not want to take over after you, but one or some surely will if you have set a good example, and you have prepared someone to be ready. Anyone that follows you should have been prepared with the information to grow as well as not make the same mistakes that you did. An apprentice should be better-equipped than the one that preceded them.

It is important to mention that it may be very beneficial for people to see how your work fits into your personal life. Without diving too deep into your private dealings, show those around you how plausible it is to have an efficient balance between work and home. That tends to become a key part in future decision-making, and seldom are people prepared to make such life-changing choices. It's also important for them to see how the pieces of your life tie in together. In doing so, it will help prevent certain behaviors by being proactive in your approach. Perfect example: you're running a nonprofit organization, and your team members have full-time jobs outside of the organization. Make it a point to discuss what it looks like to balance both.

Now you have laid the groundwork and foundation for a mentee to be able to make certain decisions because both of you are on the same page with your expectations of each other. You've already talked about timing in regards to coming to the office from work and still having enough time to go home and prepare for the next day, or as it pertains to activities done on the weekend. You already know that they will miss certain events because their children have sports games on the weekends, and now it is a nonfactor because you have already had this discussion and explained ways to manage it.

It's important to be intentional about building your followers to become leaders in their own right with the intent to multiply your impact. It's easier to teach five students than 500 students, and each of those five students can then go on to teach five more, and so on until you have grown exponentially.

Many people will not even be able to see their full potential, so in many cases, you may need to take it upon yourself to personally work to bring that out of them. You will first have to learn to notice people's potential by spending time with them. Find ways to put people you mentor into positions to force them to go above and beyond their usual effort. When you decipher what their "why" is that motivates them, use that as a catalyst to show them what they have inside of them. All of us have great power inside of us and a purpose for our lives. Some of us just need the right person to help bring it out.

Before you take it upon yourself to build someone up or to mold them, you must first nurture your own development and foster your ideas into concrete plans. The worst thing that anyone could do is to lead someone down the wrong path because they didn't have a map themselves. There is no rush to duplicate yourself. Nobody would allow you to build a second house if the first one was still under construction. All good things take time, so please take the time to focus on self-growth first. When you feel that the time is right and that you have developed a brand around you that needs to be unleashed into the world, then you can continue following the process outlined in this chapter.

This doesn't mean you have to be the president of any-thing, but I want you to be fully prepared for what is coming your way as you take the next steps to become a leader. Even if your goal isn't to start a major movement or to be an executive at a large company, being able to duplicate your success is a powerful tool. You should duplicate your success by giving anyone that needs or wants access to the knowledge that you have accumulated by sharing the same information, books, and mentors that you used to achieve your success.

Sometimes, you just want to help someone out who doesn't have all of the same information that you do. While in college, everything that I learned I would be sure to pass along to any of my friends or anyone that was willing to listen and learn. There were even times where strangers or people who had heard me speak or saw me at an event before would contact me to ask questions or get more details about a statement might have made.

As you continue to build your brand the right way, people will want to ask for guidance. You can't rush into or push to be someone's mentor; your brand will speak for itself. In most situations, people will come to you when the time is right, or when they need the help. In the alternate case, some people will need a push or may not know that they need your help yet. In any case, be prepared. Companies like Google and Apple don't need to beg people to apply for jobs at their companies because they have a solid brand with people begging them for jobs. The same goes for you. If you build a strong enough brand, people will approach you to be mentored instead of the other way around.

Success will be measured by the people you touch, and your name will be remembered by the people you impact. Be sure to invest as much into them as you invest into yourself. With the same love that you have for service, give back to someone and pay it forward so they may have it better than you did. You don't need to tangibly touch a person to help them. Books, interviews, videos, and building good leaders who build more leaders are all ways to touch people indirectly.

interviews, videos, and building good leaders who build more leaders are all ways to touch people indirectly.

Ensure your lessons can't be diluted as they trickle down

Make sure you are training everybody in the "why" as well as the "how." So many people are blindly following leaders simply because of who they are or how they feel at the moment. However, such leadership will only be able to survive a short-term. People's minds change every day, so on any given day, those same followers could just up and leave you or, turn their backs on you.

The key to leading people is to keep their faith, not in you as a person, but in the mission and purpose that you believe in. As long as their belief is in you, then their loyalty will always be susceptible to being lost. We all make mistakes; however, you are aware that everyone is not always understanding of those mistakes and are not obligated to give you a second chance.

We have all seen a situation where a leader made a blunder at home or even in the public eye and was heavily scrutinized for said error. Because of that scrutiny, everyone who had once loved and respected them has now left his side, and that loyalty and faithfulness left along with them. That is the major downfall of following a person and not a mission or purpose.

If that purpose or goal is always held paramount, then no one person will be able to have too much power over anyone or any decision. Those very same mistakes that ended the movement in the prior example can no longer be derailed with misplaced faith. As long as that mission stays authentic, then so will the people following it, and no one person could ruin or sabotage its success and continuity. With that mission's goal being authentic, as the message gets passed down to new members, it will always maintain its substance.

As your team continues to grow and new people decide to join in your pursuit of success, you will need to create a system of continuity and plug each member into it. Have you ever looked at a major corporation such as Bank of America or Microsoft and wondered how they could bring in hundreds of new employees each year and the company not fall apart? There are a few reasons for that from a team building perspective:

Each new hire experiences the same training and learns the exact same information. This eliminates any confusion of the company's the purpose, plan, and culture.

Every employee is there to do their job and aid the company. Notice that there was no mention of who they were working for or who they had to answer to. When someone gets a promotion or moves to a different part of the company, their reasoning for being there does not change.

There are multiple levels of leadership; no one person has to handle all the work nor make all of the decisions. If each person does their job the correct way, then the company will continue to thrive because each of its moving parts are working in unison.

If you model your team in a similar fashion, you will be able to run an effective and efficient group of dedicated people as well as alleviate some of the pressure, stress, and headache from your life and allow you to have fun doing what you love.

This system will include:

A thorough description of what your team or organization does. Included in this will be your mission statement and your vision as well as your plan of action over the next three to five years.

An explanation of each position and its roles.

A template for any document they may have to prepare or for any event that they will have to organize.

A detailed set of bylaws, which includes all rules, regulations, and best practices.

Your mentees should be preparing to help lead each member of your team go be getting ready to go out and lead their own teams. They should be the first people plugged into that system and should be used to help facilitate the learning for the rest of the group. These should be the people closest to you, so they should have the luxury of seeing the parts of your life that everyone else doesn't get to. In doing so, the hope is that they don't have to be told everything and the majority of what they're learning will be from experience. They can learn everything that you know just from being around you and conversing with you on topics of importance. After all, they will be the beginning and the moving force behind leaving that great legacy of yours.

CHAPTER 11

WHAT'S NEXT?

*"If your actions create a legacy that inspires others
to dream more, learn more, do more and become
more, then, you are an excellent leader."*[18]

**Now that you have all the steps, how do you put it all
into action?**

Becoming a great leader is a marathon, not a sprint. The
sooner you begin to prepare yourself, the better you'll be. It
will take time to master everything that I explained and laid
out in this book. Go chapter by chapter and try to master
each skill one at a time and start combining skills as you master them.

Leverage your network. Utilize the people that are
already around you to help you grow. There is no minimum or
maximum number of people that it takes to start practicing
how to be a better leader. Just don't be one of those people
who want to wait to do something until they have a title or until
you get to "this or that" stage of your life. If you begin doing all

of the right things now, once you receive the title that you're looking for, you will be prepared to use the new platform that comes with that new title to its maximum potential.

Find opportunities – you just have to ask. People are afraid to ask for the things that they want. You already have what it takes to attain whatever goals you have set in place, you just have to bring yourself to unleash the greatness that is within you. Don't attempt to achieve them by yourself. ASK FOR HELP! There is no shame in requesting and receiving opportunities from other people. We all have to start somewhere, so why make it harder on yourself.

I have a few of these skills already. How do I work on all of them at the same time?

You don't have to tackle all of these points at once. In fact, you shouldn't even try. Some skills will lead naturally into others, while some you may need to master before you can tackle others. It's not a race to the finish line. With hard work, each skill will come in time.

Everything is intertwined. As you search within yourself for your passion, you will start to find other people who are like-minded and start developing your network. While developing your leadership style, you will simultaneously begin to build your brand. Many of these skills will be constructed concurrently.

As you master everything, you must apply your leadership skills to whatever it is that you're good at, whether it's an office, a nonprofit, coaching, teaching, or whatever. Your goal is to weave and connect these things into the life you're already living. Continuously learning is the only way to improve your craft and duplicate yourself through your success.

What will being a leader look like?

It can be stressful having to deal with other people's lives and emotions. Some days, you might not want to be a role model, but you will need to tighten up your belt and do what you have been designed to do. You'll have days where you don't feel like it, but leadership is the path that you chose, so you can't break. You must grow firm in your resolve and stick it out through the rough days.

It will include long nights trying to come up with new ways to progress and how best to lead. It will include deep thoughts and conversations about goals and missions with others. Sometimes you need to talk to yourself about how to get better. Sometimes you need to talk to other people about how they messed up and how you guys can improve together. Sometimes you will have to take responsibility for something that was not your fault. Get used to the long conversations that are inevitable between yourself, your mentors, and your mentees.

Always contemplate the pros and cons of every decision. Your decisions affect others, so you always want to be mindful of the impact of your leadership. Life is a double-edged sword. You're going to gain and lose something in every decision you make. Is the reward that you hope to gain greater than the risk of what you could lose? If not, then don't make that decision.

People will not always follow the same path you do, and sometimes you have to sacrifice for the good of your own mission. When you're on the road less-traveled, determination and drive are going to be what fuels you to keep pushing. It is within these tough days that you will have to remember your "why," the reason that you continue to work hard. What is your "why"? Is it wanting a better life for yourself, a better life for your family and/or a better life for everyone? Maybe your goal is to honor the life of a loved one or simply a desire to be great. Whatever that reason is, stick with it and use it to motivate you.

As you continue to grow, you want to be sure that what you're doing is adding value to yourself and those around you. There should be something unique about what you do. You can't copy everybody else. If the product or service that you provide can be given from someone else, then what is making you stand out? Find what makes you stand out from the pack and utilize that. Search within yourself and your daily habits and routines and figure out what makes you unique.

That's when leadership skills become valuable. In the corporate setting, promotions are gifted to those who add value to the company. If you don't add value to the company, your opportunities for promotions will be few and far between. If you aren't doing anything out of the ordinary, you aren't bringing any extra value to the company. The same goes for outside of work. The people who continue to climb the ladder and find new opportunities are the leaders that continue to leave their unique stamp on everything they do. What makes you unique? Use it.

When I learned how to utilize my leadership ability, I had already realized that I had a passion for helping others. I created my own nonprofit, a charter school, because I took the life I was already living and just added leadership components that made my nonprofit better as a result of the skills I acquired.

Be diligent in applying the skills that you read about in this book. You CAN become the global leader you've always dreamed of becoming! The world is counting on you. I want to wish you the best of luck on your journey.

As a final note, somebody invested themselves into you, so pay it forward and invest in somebody else. A great way to start would be to gift this book to someone who you know can make a difference.

WORKS CITED

1. "What Is Leadership," Mind Tools, Accessed May 18, 2018, https://www.mindtools.com/pages/article/newLDR_41.htm.

2. Prayers Offered by the Chaplain, the Rev. Peter Marshall ... 1947–1948, p. 20 (1949). Senate Doc. 80–170

3. Napoleon Hill, *Think and Grow Rich: The Landmark Bestseller Now Revised and Updated for the 21st Century.*

4. Norman Vincent Peale, author of *The Power of Positive Thinking.*

5. John F Kennedy, inauguration speech, US Capitol, Jan. 20, 1961.

6. Jack Canfield, author of the *Chicken Soup For The Soul* books.

7. Frank Outlaw, 1977 May 18, San Antonio Light, What They're Saying, Quote Page 7-B (NArch Page 28), Column 4, San Antonio, Texas. (NewspaperArchive).

8. 1938, Morally I Roll Along by Gay MacLaren (Gay Zenola MacLaren), Section: I Meet Mark Twain, Quote Page 66, Little, Brown and Company, Boston, Massachusetts. (Verified with photocopies; thanks to Professor Charles C. Doyle and the University of Georgia library system).

9. Otto von Bismarck (1815-1898) Prussian German statesman and aristocrat.

10. "Top 10 Leadership Qualities That Make Good Leaders," Task Que, accessed May 28, 2018 https://blog.taskque.com/characteristics-good-leaders/.

11. Dwight D. Eisenhower.

12. Robert T. Kiyosaki, *Rich Dad, Poor Dad*.

13. "9 Killer Branding Quotes From The World's Top Billionaires," Addicted 2 Success, Jeff Bezos, accessed June 11, 2018 https://addicted2success.com/quotes/9-killer-branding-quotes-from-the-worlds-top-billionaires/.

14. John Martin, personal interview?

15. Raki McGregor, personal interview?

16. Margaret Mead.

17. Keith Cockrell, personal interview?

18. Dolly Parton, The *Most Important Thing I Know*.

ADDITIONAL SOURCES

1. "What Are Your Values," Mind Tools, Accessed May 24, 2018, https://www.mindtools.com/pages/article/newTED_85.htm

2. "Core Values List," James Clear, Accessed May 24, 2018, https://jamesclear.com/core-values

3. "Core Values List: Over 200 Personal Values to Discover What's Most Important to You," Scott Jeffrey, Accessed May 24, 2018, https://scottjeffrey.com/core-values-list/

4. Life Straw, accessed May 31, 2018, https://www.lifestraw.com/

5. Toastmasters International https://www.toastmasters.org/

FURTHER READING

1. *Rich Dad Poor Dad*

2. *Think And Grow Rich*

3. *Never Eat Alone*